Partnering with Parents

Partnering with Parents

Boosting Literacy for All Ages

Mary Schreiber

An Imprint of ABC-CLIO, LLC

Santa Barbara, California • Denver, Colorado

Library of Congress Cataloging-in-Publication Data

Names: Schreiber, Mary, author.
Title: Partnering with parents : boosting literacy for all ages / Mary Schreiber.
Description: Santa Barbara, California : Libraries Unlimited, an Imprint
    of ABC-CLIO, LLC, [2019] | Includes bibliographical references and index.
Identifiers: LCCN 2019006538 (print) | LCCN 2019008244 (ebook) |
    ISBN 9781440863936 (ebook) | ISBN 9781440863929 (paperback :
    acid-free paper)
Subjects: LCSH: Children—Books and reading. | Reading—Parent participation.
Classification: LCC LB1050 (ebook) | LCC LB1050 .S287 2019 (print) |
    DDC 649/.58—dc23
LC record available at https://lccn.loc.gov/2019006538

ISBN: 978-1-4408-6392-9 (paperback)
      978-1-4408-6393-6 (ebook)

23 22 21 20 19   1 2 3 4 5

This book is also available as an ebook.

Libraries Unlimited
An Imprint of ABC-CLIO, LLC

ABC-CLIO, LLC
147 Castilian Drive
Santa Barbara, California 93117
www.abc-clio.com

This book is printed on acid-free paper ∞

Manufactured in the United States of America

For Mom, Dad, Molly, Dave, Matt, Allison, and Corinne

Contents

Acknowledgments

I would like to acknowledge all of the libraries, and their staff, who were willing to share the inspiring work that they do. Your talents will help others expand their efforts to help parents and children discover the magic of reading. I would not have a book without you.

A big thank-you to Wendy Bartlett, for encouraging me to write this book. You were wonderful about cheering me on, keeping me focused, and answering my questions about the publishing process.

A special thank-you to my mother, Gayle Schreiber. As a retired educator and school librarian, with over 30 years of experience, you have shared your wisdom and knowledge about literacy and the learning-to-read process with me my whole life. You truly were my first teacher and I am still learning from you every day. Thanks for being the first reader of *Partnering with Parents*.

Introduction

If you have picked up this book, you are hopefully looking for ways to expand the collections, programs, and services for families that you offer in your public or school library. My goal in writing this book is to give you the tools you need to provide even better support to the parents and children you serve.

You will not become a reading teacher from reading this book, but after reading, you should have a better understanding of the challenges both parents and children experience on the path to being independent readers. You may or may not remember this process from your own childhood. If you do remember, it might be a fond memory or it could be one you wish you could forget. No matter the experience, you came out on the other side, and now you can help the families in your community do the same.

There are a couple of words used throughout the book that I would like to further define. One word is "parent" or "caregiver." I recognize that there are lots of adults in a child's life and they may have a huge impact on a child's reading success without necessarily having the title of mother or father. Using the word "parent" or "caregiver" is not meant to diminish the role these additional caring adults have. Both the terms "parent" and "caregiver" represent caring adults that may include foster parents, stepparents, grandparents, aunts and uncles, neighbors, friend's parents, and teachers.

The other term is "librarian," and it can mean anyone who is working with kids in the library. It does not necessarily need to be someone with a master's in library science degree. The programs and tips throughout this book are meant for all library workers who want to help boost literacy.

Organization

You can read this book straight through or you can go directly to the chapters that are of most interest to you. The concepts do build upon each other to a certain extent, but, depending on your current knowledge, you can skip around a little more freely.

Chapter 1 focuses on early literacy. You will find tips to share with parents, types of books to become familiar with, and programs and services that bring the library out into the community.

Chapter 2 delves into the importance of play. You may not think about play and literacy together, but the two really do go hand in hand. Learn about sourcing out toys and apps. Discover programs that promote play and literacy at the same time.

Chapter 3 looks at when the reading process begins. A big piece that parents will need support around is the leveling of books. Learn how other libraries are helping parents find the right books for their child and programs that support the learning-to-read process.

Chapter 4 removes the word "struggling reader" and instead focuses on the "developing reader." These kids may be seen as behind the normal track for learning to read, but with the right support and encouragement from schools, libraries, and parents, they can excel.

Chapter 5 examines the ways to encourage reluctant or apathetic readers into becoming enthusiastic readers. Find programs and book formats that can help make this happen.

Chapter 6 looks at the school age child and how libraries can support these parents and kids by offering exciting programs that include literacy aspects beyond just reading.

Chapter 7 asks you to examine your library's space, collection, and programming with inclusivity in mind. Many times, you are not as diverse or inclusive as you strive to be. Taking a step back and looking at where you are and where you want to be can help you achieve your goals.

Chapter 8 finds ways to keep parents and families engaged with reading and the library as the kids get older. Using the library together and sharing books does not have to end when kids enter middle school or even high school.

The Epilogue explains that the goal of this book is not that you will adopt every program or service discussed. Libraries are busier than ever with all the different programs and services being offered. Instead, the hope is that you will use the ideas found here as an inspiration to tweak programs you already offer or pick a couple to slowly add into your workflow. No matter what, to be a literacy expert you need to read, and you need to read lots, and you need to read widely.

CHAPTER ONE

Helping Parents Get It Right from the Beginning

Libraries have been connecting with parents and providing storytime for generations. In the early 2000s, the Public Library Association and the Association of Library Service to Children, two divisions of the American Library Association, joined together to study how to incorporate early literacy skills into workshops for caregivers and daycare providers and into traditional storytime programs that public libraries offer. As defined by the Cedar Mill Community Libraries website, "Early Literacy is what children know about reading and writing *before* they actually read or write" (Cedar Mill Community Libraries, Early Literacy 2017).

Fundamentals of Early Literacy

Just as this initiative was getting under way, I started my first children's library job as an assistant in the Children's Department of the Parma Heights Branch of Cuyahoga County Public Library, Ohio. During those first few months, I was trained on the storytime best practices for Cuyahoga County Public Library. We were doing traditional storytimes for babies, toddlers, and preschoolers. The emphasis was on songs, rhymes, repetition, and age-appropriate books.

At the time, I was the most nervous about conducting storytimes with parents in the room. Who was I, a twenty-something with no children of my own, to tell parents how to interact with their baby? I definitely had a fear of making a fool of myself in front of the parents or saying the wrong thing.

Of course, the first program I was asked to do when I was hired was the Baby and Me Storytime. There I was with a group of mostly mothers and their babies. I quickly learned that the caregivers were really happy to be there. They wanted to connect with other adults and wanted their babies to meet other babies. Not every parent knows nursery rhymes or the motions librarians model to go with the words. Even though I was the newbie in the room, I did have an expertise that I could share. I practiced up on my nursery rhymes, found music that I could sing along to, and discovered the board books that worked well when shared with a group.

All of this was great and the parents and babies were enjoying the program, but there was no explanation for the parents on why we were doing what we were doing. While it was fun, we were not making it clear to the adults that sharing rhymes and reading together builds skills necessary for school and reading success down the line. That's where Every Child Ready to Read came in.

Every Child Ready to Read, Part I

Every Child Ready to Read was just being introduced to the children's staff at my library system when I was promoted to a children's librarian. The original intention of the Every Child Ready to Read creators may have been that library staff conduct parent and daycare teacher workshops, but public libraries were also deciding to add these elements into weekly storytimes. The focus on storytime at Cuyahoga County Public Library was shifting to incorporating the six literacy skills. I agreed with why we needed to be more intentional in our practices, but I found the parent instruction pieces difficult to get used to. It took a while to find the right rhythm for going from rhyme or book to parent snippet.

I never read off my program planning sheet but instead used it as my crutch to make sure I was following the new best practices. It allowed me to better share early literacy information with caregivers in the areas of vocabulary, print motivation, print awareness, narrative skills, letter knowledge, and phonological awareness.

Every Child Ready to Read, Part II

Shortly after I left working at a branch and moved into the collection development department, Every Child Ready to Read got a refresh and now focuses on five key areas of practice—sing, talk, read, write, and play, in conjunction with the previous six literacy skills. It still includes many things libraries were already doing with families, but now there are even more types of information to share and model with parents. For example, some librarians started using magnetic boards with letters to have kids help them spell out the weekly theme in preschool storytime, an activity that caregivers could easily continue at home. Appendix A has a sample storytime that incorporates both the six literacy skills and the five areas of practice.

Family Engagement

Whether you adopt the principles of Every Child Ready to Read or not, it is critical that you embrace the idea of family engagement at your library. Programs for the very young must include parent involvement, and this does not just mean programs for babies and toddlers. Caregivers need to be present in preschool storytimes too. Modeling reading aloud and literacy best practices does not end when a child turns three.

Some might make the case that a child needs the separation time from their parents. I disagree with this premise because attending storytime together is a way for the family unit to bond. While it might be a shift in practice to invite caregivers into a preschool storytime, it is very rewarding for parents to see the continued development their child makes in the areas of literacy and other education concepts, including early math skills, over the course of their storytime attendance.

Taking it a step further, to engage the whole family, it is important for libraries to offer programs for the *whole* family. These family storytimes provide an opportunity for siblings to attend storytime together and, for busy parents, a chance for their children to attend storytime each week which they otherwise might not be able to if they had to come on different days or times. I once had a mother who had the grandmother come to hang out with her toddler, while she took the baby to storytime. She was lucky to have a mother able to do this. However, once I realized this was happening, I invited the grandmother and the sibling to attend with the mother and the baby. Eventually, it was just the mother and the two kids and that was fine. For other families, having an extra adult or finding a babysitter to stay home with siblings probably is not an option. Without a program for infants through preschool age children or the willingness to bend a little on letting siblings into a storytime, these kids might miss out.

If you are unsure what to offer for a family storytime, here are some tried and true tips to help you out. First, have extra book choices because the age makeup of the group may change from week to week. I like to have a couple of board books, a couple of shorter picture books, and a couple of picture books that I would normally share with preschoolers. That way I have lots of books to choose from and can select titles that best match the attention span of the group that week. Start with the longest books first, as a child's ability to listen will diminish over time. This is a good tip to share with caregivers about book choices for snuggle reading time at home.

Second, like toddler storytime, I include lots of movement in family storytime. It is fun to get parents and siblings up and dancing around to the music. Third, use repetition of rhymes as a way to demonstrate the best movements and motions for a specific age group. One example would be the classic "Noble Duke of York." When I do this with babies, the parents hold the babies and bounce and lift. I call it their workout for the day. With toddlers and preschoolers who are walking, they can practice marching in place and standing up and crouching down. Parents can assist as needed or participate by doing the movements with their child. As long as you are including caregivers in each part of the program and modeling ways for all ages to participate, you will find that families will keep coming back.

Collection Development and Merchandising: Young Child

One of the fastest-growing markets in the juvenile book world is board books. In the retail market the percentage of board books sales has been on the increase, and it was up by 11 percent in 2017 when compared to 2016 sales (Milliot 2018). It is great to know that parents and caring adults are willing to shell out money to purchase books for the children in their lives.

The problem is that those caring adults may be purchasing ones that are above their child's attention span or comprehension. The unintended result may be a reading experience that is frustrating for both the parent and the child. The baby, toddler, or preschooler may become bored if the topic is too advanced or the book has too many words per page. I'm always cautious of board books that were originally published as picture books. Most of the time the publisher has not asked the author to make any changes to the text, and it will be too long and difficult for a baby or toddler to comprehend. Dropping this fact into conversations with parents can help them make better book choices.

Caregivers who don't have an early childhood education or a children's librarian background are not always going to have the selection knowledge to determine the age-appropriateness of a book. And this is where librarians can make a real difference. Along with sharing and building the skills of Every Child Ready to Read during storytime, we can model and discuss with parents what makes a great book for their child based on that child's age and interest. Sounds familiar? Yes, this is the readers advisory interview that we do with kids who are able to communicate with us, usually preschool and older. With the under-three set, the discussion needs to happen with the parents. Some phrases I have used with caregivers in storytime include:

- Sturdy pages in a board book make it easier for your baby and toddler to turn the pages. Helping with book time aids in developing a sense that reading is an enjoyable and important activity.

- If your child loses interest while reading, it's okay to stop. Attention spans are short at this age. Reading should be fun, not a chore for either the child or the parent.

- When graduating to picture books, make sure to look for ones that have lots of pictures and only a few words per page.

- If your child likes trains, read about trains. If your child likes cats, read about cats. Books about topics that interest your child are bound to make them ask to hear them again and again.

- Looking for a way to cut down on the number of toy presents at birthdays and holidays? Suggest to family and friends that they bring a book instead. Librarians are happy to make recommendations!

Formats for Early Childhood Books

Public libraries will have collections of both board books and picture books for families to read together. A school library will typically not serve the youngest age group, but, like a public library, it should still include a collection of more complex picture books that will appeal to elementary and middle school readers.

Board Books

Sharing board books with babies is crucial. An excellent board book will draw the attention of the very young, and they will sit still long enough to hear the very limited story. There may also be no story, and, if that is the case, parents need to be comfortable sharing the word on the page and pointing out things about the image to their baby or toddler.

This collection needs to be weeded often as teething tots will likely use board books to chew on. This is part of the cost of doing business, and when they come back a little worse for wear, I would not charge parents for a damaged book. By letting this go, you are encouraging continued use by families instead of making them afraid to check out books.

When I get new board books, I like to bring them into my baby and toddler storytimes and create a small display in the room. Parents appreciate being the first to check out a book, and it is a great opportunity to handsel the titles you are most excited about. New board books that do not get checked out during storytime should be displayed with the rest of your new book collection and not simply shelved in your board book section. At one of my branches, the parents rarely will browse the board book area, but, if the books are displayed and look like new, they will circulate. Learn to pay attention to your families' browsing habits and put your displays in their path.

Picture Books

Little hands that are used to the sturdiness of board pages might need some time to get used to the fragility of a picture book's thin paper. With picture books try to show some restraint; do not tape up torn pages and never use a book that has taped pages in storytime. This may sound sacrilegious, but the more pristine a book looks, the more likely it will be checked out by parents. Like with board books, I would try to be flexible on fees for damaged picture books. Exploring books leads to enjoyment, and you do not want to throw up unnecessary barriers.

Face-out display, especially of picture books, really helps to sell them to families. Display your newest and most popular together. You can do this on a table or other display fixture if you have the room and the furniture to do it. If not, a great alternative is to free up some shelving at the entrance to your space. Then simply fill it with lots of face-out picture books and remember to refill throughout the day—especially before and after storytimes and other children's programs.

If your library has book bins rather than shelves for the picture book collection, you will want to make sure the hottest titles are on the top as they will be face out and easy for kids and caregivers to flip through. You will also want to consider moving titles from the bottom to the top periodically to give book bin sitters a better chance of being checked out. People tend to browse the top of the book bins and only look to the bottoms if they are seeking a specific title.

Getting to Know the Collection

To help parents get excited about books, it is important to find ones that will engage both the parent and the child. Here are some types of books and specific examples that are sure to be crowd-pleasers.

A Child's World

Babies love to look at other babies in books. The best option is to find ones with photos of babies. Illustrations of babies also work, and if there is a mirror element you cannot go wrong. As kids grow the books that are read to them should continue to show them images of children.

Ellwand, David. **The Big Book of Beautiful Babies.** New York, NY: Dutton Children's Books, 2001 (1995). unpaged. $8.99. 9780525465461.
Diverse photos of babies doing everyday things and expressing simple emotions. Includes a mirror page at the end so babies can see themselves. (Board Book)

Fox, Mem. **Ten Little Finger and Ten Little Toes.** Illustrated by Helen Oxenbury. Orlando, FL: Harcourt, Inc., 2008. unpaged. $16.00. 9780152060572.
> Babies are born in places all over the world, but they have many things in common including their cute fingers and toes. (Picture Book)

Katz, Karen. **Kiss Baby's Boo-Boo.** New York, NY: Little Simon, 2016. unpaged. $6.99. 9781481442084.
> Lift the flaps to see the diverse babies getting licks from pets and kisses by family members to make them feel better. Katz is a prolific writer, and all of her titles are great choices. (Board Book)

Rogge, Robie. **Baby See, Baby Do.** Illustrated by Jennifer Hale. San Francisco, CA: Chronicle Books, LLC, 2018. unpaged. $9.99. 9781452168906.
> Babies can practice recognizing emotions in the photographed babies as well as look at their own expressions in the mirror that is attached as a flap. (Board Book)

Spanyol, Jessica. **Clive and His Babies.** Swindon, UK: Child's Play International Ltd., 2016. unpaged. (All About Clive). $4.99. 9781846438820.
> Clive has many adventures, but, in this book, he is taking care of his dolls. These books defy gender stereotypes. (Board Book)

Tabby, Abigail. **Welcome Home, Baby!** Illustrated by Sam Williams. New York, NY: Little Simon, 2017. unpaged. (New Books for Newborns). $7.99. 9781534401037.
> This book is more for the caregivers. It takes the family through the moments that happen when a new baby comes home for the first time. (Board Book)

Thompson, Carol. **Dance.** Swindon, UK: Childs Play International Ltd., 2017. unpaged. (Amazing Me!). $4.99. 9781846439599.
> Thompson does a great job of creating participatory books for the youngest of children. (Board Book)

Van Camp, Richard. **We Sang You Home.** Illustrated by Julie Flett. Victoria, BC: Orca Book Publishers, 2016. unpaged. $9.95. 9781459811782.
> First Nation parents express the love they have for their new baby. (Board Book)

Concept Books

Reading and math are two subjects that will be super important during the school years. Alphabet, shape, and number concept books are a great way to help build these skills starting from infancy. A cool thing about basic shape books is that it helps babies and toddlers to recognize letters later on. I love sharing this tidbit with caregivers as they are always surprised to learn it. What I recommend you look for are books that tell a story well, rather than just teach a concept when sharing with preschoolers. They are the most fun to be shared in storytime and for parents to share one-on-one with their child.

Baker, Keith. **LMNO Peas.** New York, NY: Beach Lane Books, 2010. unpaged. $16.99. 9781416991410.

    Vocabulary is taught along with the letters of the alphabet as kids learn all kinds of jobs they can have when they grow up. (Picture Book)

Khan, Hena. **Crescent Moons and Pointed Minarets: A Muslim Book of Shapes**. Illustrated by Mehrdokht Amini. San Francisco, CA: Chronicle Books, 2018. unpaged. $17.99. 9781452155418.

    Going beyond the basic shapes, children will experience the Muslim world through the shapes that make it, for example, arches, octagons, and cubes. (Picture Book)

Martin, Bill, Jr., and John Archambault Jr. **Chicka Chicka Boom Boom.** Illustrated by Lois Ehlert. New York, NY: Simon & Schuster Books for Young Readers, 1989. unpaged. $17.99. 9780671679491.

    A classic story of alphabet letters climbing a coconut tree. This book was originally published in 1989, so it is likely to strike a chord with parents and grandparents if you share it in storytime. (Picture Book)

Schoonmaker, Elizabeth. **Square Cat ABC.** New York, NY: Aladdin, 2014. unpaged. $15.99. 9781442498952.

    A simple garden story told with each letter of the alphabet making an appearance. (Picture Book)

Tamaki, Jillian. **They Say Blue.** New York, NY: Abrams Books for Young Readers, 2018. unpaged. $17.99. 9781419728518.

    A young girl uses colors to explore nature and the seasons. Save this one to share with preschoolers and kindergarteners. (Picture Book)

Twohy, Mike. **Oops Pounce Quick Run!: An Alphabet Caper.** New York, NY: Balzer + Bray, 2016. unpaged. $17.99. 9780062377005.

    A bouncing ball starts it all! With only one word per page, this book tells a clever story that children want to hear multiple times. (Picture Book)

Walsh, Ellen Stoll. **Mouse Shapes.** Orlando, FL: Harcourt, Inc., 2007. unpaged. $16.99. 9780152060916.

    The narrative will teach children how shapes fit together to make other shapes. (Picture Book)

High Contrast

For very young children, books with high contrast between the colors will make it easier to focus and see the images. These are a few that really stand out.

Foster, Jane. **Jane Foster's Black and White.** New York, NY: Little Bee Books, 2016. unpaged. $7.99. 9781499802559.

    White words on black backgrounds show an animal name and a describing action word. On the opposite page find black-and-white animals on colored backgrounds. (Board Book)

Hoban, Tana. **Black White.** New York, NY: Greenwillow Books, 2017 (1993). unpaged. $8.99. 9780062656902.

A wordless collection of shape outlines for babies and parents to discover and discuss. This one is a classic that was first published in 1993. (Board Book)

Priddy, Roger. **Words: A High Contrast Board Book.** Illustrated by Holly Jackman. New York, NY: Priddy Books, 2013. unpaged. (Hello Baby). $4.99. 9780312515980.

The colors go beyond black and white but remain strong contrasts. The text and illustrations are limited to one word and the object described. (Board Book)

Movement

One of the five practices of Every Child Ready to Read, Part 2 is movement. Developing this skill is important to the development of coordination as related to gross and fine motor skills. Songs and other aspects of a traditional storytime will encourage movement, but so can a book like the ones mentioned next. A book that suggests dancing or that you can act out is a great pick for demonstrating to caregivers how they can incorporate movement into reading and play at home.

Boynton, Sandra. **Let's Dance, Little Pookie.** New York, NY: Little Simon, 2017. unpaged. (Sandra Boynton's Pookie Books!). $5.99. 9781481497725.

Piggie mommy and baby are boogieing! The text is perfect at encouraging the parent reader and the child listener to join in the fun. This is just one of Boynton's classic tales. (Board Book)

Carle, Eric. **From Head to Toe.** New York, NY: HarperCollins Publishers, 1997. unpaged. $17.99. 9780060235154.

Children can exercise along with their favorite animal friends. (Picture Book)

Montanari, Susan McElroy. **Hip-Hop Lollipop.** Illustrated by Brian Pinkney. New York, NY: Schwartz & Wade Books, 2018. unpaged. $17.99. 9781101934821.

Lollipop just can't stop moving! She does hip-hop all the way to bed. (Picture Book)

Sims, Stacy. **Baby Loves to Wiggle Wiggle.** Illustrated by Sharareh Khosravani. Cincinnati, OH: Blue Manatee Press, 2017. unpaged. $7.99. 9781936669578.

Diverse families are playing with the baby and the text models how parents can interact with their own child. (Board Book)

Reluctant Parent Readers

Not every person who becomes a parent likes to read books that are written for young children. Parents may find the simplicity of the stories boring even when they know the importance of reading them to their baby. If that is the case, these books might just be what you need to help bridge the adult book world with the kid's book world.

Board books in general are a growing market, and these books that are meant to appeal to parents and grandparents are cropping up more and more. I resisted a little at first, but after several requests from staff and customers I broke down and picked up the Cozy Classics series and they have circulated well. A definite appeal to literature lovers.

When the science board books arrived on the scene, I immediately purchased. These have been very popular with our techy parents and with some of the parents who work at NASA. My tip is to not be afraid to add some trendy books to your circulating collection, especially if your customers are clamoring for them.

Adams, Jennifer. **A Little Princess: A Friendship Primer.** Illustrated by Alison Oliver. Layton, UT: Gibbs Smith Publisher, 2017. unpaged. (BabyLit). $9.99. 9781423645955.
  Very simplified retelling of classic stories. (Board Book)
Brantz, Loryn. **Feminist Baby.** New York, NY: Disney Hyperion, 2017. unpaged. $12.99. 9781484778586.
  Fun illustrations and short sentences explore just what a girl can like and be—anything. (Board Book)
Ferrie, Chris. **Quantum Entanglement for Babies.** Naperville, IL: Sourcebooks Jabberwocky, 2014. unpaged. (Baby University). $9.99. 9781492656234.
  Complex science concepts are streamlined to create books that are sure to appeal to science nerds and the babies in their lives. (Board Book)
Perkins, Chloe. **Cinderella.** Illustrated by Sandra Equihua. New York, NY: Little Simon, 2016. unpaged. (Once Upon a World). $8.99. 9781481479158.
  Classic fairytales are shortened and populated with a diverse cast of characters. (Board Book)
Wang, Jack, and Holman Wang. **Jane Austen's Emma.** San Francisco, CA: Chronicle Books LLC., 2016 (2013). unpaged. (Cozy Classics). $9.95. 9781452152554.
  Classics are abridged to one word per page. Photos of felt creations portray the word and together they pay homage to the original work. (Board Book)

Repetition

Repeating words and phrases help build a child's confidence to assist with telling a story. Books that rhyme or that offer repetition of sentences are likely to be some of the first ones that will help a young child learn to read. It is crucial that caregivers understand that these first successes with stories are the building blocks to learning to read later.

Long, Loren. **There's a Hole in the Log on the Bottom of the Lake.** New York, NY: Philomel Books, 2018. unpaged. $17.99. 9780399163999.
  With each new item stacked on the hole in the log, the refrain gets a little longer. (Picture Book)

Mora, Oge. **Thank You, Omu!** New York, NY: Little, Brown and Company, 2018. unpaged. $18.99. 9780316431248.
> Omu is making stew and it smells so good that it brings members of her neighborhood to her door. Kids will have fun repeating the phrases "knock knock," "oh stew," and "thank you, Omu." (Picture Book)

Reynolds, Aaron. **Dude!** Illustrated by Dan Santat. New York, NY: A Neal Porter Book, 2018. unpaged. $17.99. 9781626726031.
> A sure confidence booster for kids as there is only one word in the whole story, dude, and it is repeated over and over again. A great book for practicing reading with expression. (Picture Book)

Rinker, Sherri Duskey. **Goodnight, Goodnight, Construction Site.** Illustrated by Tom Lichtenheld. San Francisco, CA: Chronicle Books, 2011. unpaged. $16.99. 9780811877824.
> The construction site gets ready for bed, and kids can help put each vehicle to sleep by repeating the refrain that appears every few pages. (Picture Book)

Rhymes and Songs

The rhythm and rhyming that goes along with songs and nursery rhymes start building a child's vocabulary at a young age and helps develop a playful relationship with language.

Fronis, Aly. **The Chicks in the Barn.** Illustrated by Jannie Ho. New York, NY: Little Bee Books, 2018. unpaged. $7.99. 9781499804836.
> Set to the tune of "The Wheels on the Bus," this farmyard story is a perfect book to introduce to families during storytime. (Board Book)

Huang, Yu-Hsuan. **Row, Row, Row Your Boat.** Somerville, MA: Nosy Crow, 2017 (2015). unpaged. (Sing Along with Me!). $8.99. 9780763692407.
> An adaption of the traditional song with an added bonus of moveable parts. (Board Book)

Opie, Iona. **On the Go with Mother Goose.** Illustrated by Rosemary Wells. Somerville, MA: Candlewick Press, 2017 (1996). unpaged. $8.99. 9780763692148.
> Some familiar and potentially unfamiliar rhymes for parents to become acquainted with. (Board Book)

Maintaining the Storytime Collection

I'm a firm believer in finding a balance between classic favorites and books that have just been published, when choosing my storytime books. Many of the libraries I have worked at have had professional collections made up of storytime reference books. This is a great way to make sure you have a clean copy of a book you love sharing with families year after year. However, you will need to go through the storytime reference collection at least once a year and weed out any books not used by staff in the last two years. An added bonus is that it makes room for the addition of new titles.

When using a reference copy of an older book, check to see if circulating copies are still available. If it is not, is the book still in print? A quick check of your book vendor's site or an e-mail to your material's selector can answer this question. I would discourage you from using books that are out of print. If you really like the book, and you can get some replacement circulating copies, go ahead and keep using. If you cannot, then it is time to retire that particular book. Without circulating copies, you prevent caregivers from being able to check out a copy to take home.

Reaching Families with Young Children

Children's librarians know all about the importance of reading aloud to babies from birth, but getting the message to non-library-using parents can be a challenge. Not only are these families not benefiting from the vast resources the library has to offer, but they are many times completely unaware that a program for babies even exists.

My hope is to see some of this shift in the next decade as the parents having children and the new grandparents will be from a generation where baby storytimes have always been a part of library service. I would like to see that the expectation be not that you start library storytimes at two or three years old but during a baby's first few months. Much can be gained by getting families into the library in those first two years when children's brain development is so critical.

New Baby Literacy Liaison—Cuyahoga County Public Library and MetroHealth Hospital, Main Campus Medical Center, Ohio

Nicole Joy Beleske coordinates volunteers for Cuyahoga County Public Library, and Becky Moldover is the director of volunteer services at Metro-Health Hospital. Together they have created a partnership that helps parents with new babies to get information about the importance of early literacy and the support the public library can provide.

Background

Around the year 2000, new baby packets were first launched at Cuyahoga County Public Library. This was roughly the same time when baby storytimes were being introduced for infants up to 18 months of age. The baby packets were cute and colorful and contained items like a collection of printed rhymes, a growth chart, and a list of branch locations. These were printed with the help of a sponsor, and the packets were given out to new parents who were seen visiting the library or at an outreach event. It was a way to quickly share the benefits of reading and rhyming with a new baby.

A second version was created around 2003, but it was still primarily used in-house, which, unfortunately, had a limited reach to new parents who were not library users already.

That all changed in 2015 when a third variation of the new baby packet was created and a new partnership was launched. Since September 2015, new baby packets have been distributed in a more direct way with volunteers visiting parents while they are still in the hospital after the birth of a child.

These visits are kept very brief, but the parents receive the new baby packet that currently includes the following:

- Booklet of rhymes to share with baby
- Paperback copy of *Read to Your Bunny* by Rosemary Wells
- My Health Diary booklet for parents to keep track of milestones
- Growth chart
- Book suggestion list along with the six early literacy skills
- Card with information on social and emotional development
- Magnet for adding emergency contact information
- Copy of *Babybug* magazine
- Cuyahoga County Public Library's Toy Library bookmark
- Library card and bookmark with library branch and hour information

The volunteer will talk about each piece of the packet and then leave it with the parents. The goal is to introduce parents to the library but not overwhelm them with tons of new information. The hope is that parents will learn a little more about what the library has to offer, the importance of reading to their infant, and eventually come to the library to activate the library card included in the packet.

The Volunteer Piece

For this program to work, there must be volunteers in place to make connections to families when babies are born. A key piece is that all families with a new baby get a visit, not just families having their first child. Interestingly enough, parents adding a second or third child to their family are sometimes more attentive than first-time parents. They get excited about the special library card, and many are surprised to learn the library has a toy-lending library.

Hiring Volunteers. All adults are invited to volunteer, and they do not need any type of degree or prior experience. However, Beleske and Moldover have found that those with an interest or background in literacy, education, or library work tend to stick around longer. They believe it is because they have a passion for reading that leads to a stronger commitment. When there is a need for a new volunteer, the opening is posted on both the library and hospital's websites. The actual applications go to Moldover at the hospital who then handles screening candidates and training them to work in a hospital setting.

The commitment is for a couple of hours, one day a week, but people have to be willing to go through the lengthy process of getting on staff and be willing to work the days and times that the hospital requires. This can sometimes be tricky for college students and retirees. They want to help but may want more flexible scheduling than can be accommodated. Moldover says that volunteers tend to either have found their niche or "self-select out" when they discover the program isn't quite what they expected.

Daily Details. MetroHealth's magic number of volunteers is three, and they rotate with one person there every other day. This allows the volunteers to see just about every new family. If they had someone every day, there just would not be enough for them to do. The volunteers are at the hospital for about one and a half to two hours per shift, and they meet with 10 to 20 families during that time. Depending on how busy the hospital you partner with, the number of volunteers and days and hours worked would vary.

When volunteers arrive, they check in at the hospital's volunteer office. It is where badges and new baby packets are picked up. Volunteers log the number of library cards given out, and this tally is given to the hospital volunteer staff who send the number to Beleske. When the library cards are activated, branch circulation staff are charged with keeping track by placing information in the library card holder's record. This allows the library to calculate how many packets were given out versus how many library cards were activated.

Parent Involvement

Parents are certainly allowed to opt out of a visit if they prefer; otherwise, they will get a short visit. If a baby is having a rough day, the nurses may tell the volunteers that it is not a good time for the family. The only other exception is the neonatal intensive care babies. It is truly about finding the sweet spot between sharing early literacy information and being sensitive to the situation at hand. And, on the positive side, the nurses enjoy and support having the volunteers on the floor. The nurses are instrumental in making the visit between volunteers and parents a success.

During the first four months of the program, September through December 2015, 200 babies were visited. In 2016, it was 813 babies and, in 2017, it was 588, which was down a little. Some of the 2017 decline is attributed to the fact that the hospital was without a volunteer staff member for two months.

What's Next

The volunteer coordinators are working on the best way to make sure the new baby packets and information shared, like the library card, aren't getting lost among all the other paraphernalia that comes home with a baby from the hospital. Always looking to improve, a couple of changes they are considering include giving the library card piece at an early wellness visit or having the doctor inquire at the visit to see if parents have had a chance to activate the card yet. This might be the prompt some parents need to dig out the forgotten card.

Adapting for Your Library

Both Moldover and Beleske are volunteer coordinators, but they work on many programs for their organizations, not just the New Baby Literacy Liaison program. Beleske oversees approximately 400 volunteers for Cuyahoga County Public Library. That said, the coordinators for a project like this could be a staff member you already have. You just might need to do a little shifting of duties to make it possible.

The bigger issue is the expense to fund the creation of the new baby packets to be distributed. This does not come out of Cuyahoga County Public Library's regular budget but instead a grant funder or sponsor is sought. If you do not have funding to create a packet or a stream of funding from another source, a packet may be out of the question. A simpler option may be to print a doubled-sided sheet with a few basic facts about early literacy on one side and storytimes at your library on the other. One more piece of paper could be a library card application. This would be a lot more cost effective and could still have a big impact if you can get them into the hands of new parents.

Partnering with a hospital or pediatrician is the ideal way to do this. You may or may not be able to help with the securing of volunteers, but if you can get the local hospital on board, you can ask that it includes the paper packet with the materials sent home with new babies. Not as ideal as a person going over the information but you would be able to reach new parents whom you would otherwise not have access to.

If working with a hospital or doctor is simply not possible, another option would be to place these print packets near the parenting titles in your collection. This is a great chance to catch the eye of new parents-to-be who are looking for parenting advice. Do not be afraid to start small and see how it goes!

Storytime at the Mall—Cuyahoga County Public Library, Ohio, North Olmsted Branch

Getting outside the four walls of the library to offer programs in the community is another way you can reach new families. Children's staff are likely making trips to daycare centers and preschools to offer storytimes. These are excellent ways to reach kids but not so great at reaching caregivers. Other avenues to explore are doing storytimes and programs at community events and spaces. You could try a farmer's market or the grocery store. Or, as one Cuyahoga County Public Library Branch does, at the mall.

Background

The North Olmsted Branch started doing a Pop-Up Library at a local farmer's market to increase its presence in the community. At these weekly visits, the library had items for checking out but they were not offering programs. However, the woman who runs the farmer's market also happens to be on the mall's advisory board. As the mall looked to become more community-minded and not just retail-oriented, she immediately thought of the local library to be a partner for the new store front that was being converted. She reached out to branch manager Andrew Harant, who worked with his staff to get the partnership off the ground.

What's Involved in the Partnership

The library is responsible for three things related to the community space at the mall. The first is to provide books for a book nook. These books are for all age levels and are copies that are checked out on a special card for the space. Visitors cannot check them out and are supposed to read them in the space. However, if someone takes a book home, the hope is that it will be returned at a later date. If not, the library is okay with that as the titles sent to the book nook are not the newest or the most popular in the collection.

The second and third items the mall asked for were related to programming. The book discussion for adults has evolved to being a chat about books rather than a regular book discussion. Coffee is provided and an adult librarian is on hand to facilitate once a month. The other program is a storytime that takes place in the space on the third Tuesday of each month, and the mall provides a snack. The storytime draws an average of eight kids plus caregivers.

Defining Roles

Children's librarian Liza Kahoe Arthur does most of the storytimes at the mall. Early on, she had to clarify who was responsible for handling any potential food allergies related to the snack. It was decided that since the mall was providing the food it would take on the liability. There is still the occasional challenge related to having snacks when the mall employee gives them to the children at the start of the storytime. This makes the active parts of the program more difficult. Kahoe Arthur continues to work with the staff to make snack time the activity that happens after the stamp at the end.

Benefits for the Library

The positives have truly balanced out any bumps along the way. Offering storytime at the mall has allowed the North Olmsted Branch staff to connect with families they do not see in the library. The diversity of participants also more closely reflects the community. Overtime, Kahoe Arthur has found that some of her library storytime families will also attend the storytime at the mall, but she is also seeing new families at the mall who are not regular library users.

Trying It Out for Yourself

One advantage of storytime at another location like the mall is that you can use the storytime plan you have already created. Kahoe Arthur finds that it really takes little additional preparation. From my experience, some things you will want to have in your go bag will include a device with the music you want to play, such as your phone, a tablet, or an old iPod. You'll also want a portable speaker so that you can turn up the volume as needed. Make sure you have a stamp and stamp pad. Once you start this tradition, kids will be disappointed if you forget.

A portable flannel board is a must if the room does not have one. Depending on how far you have to lug materials to get to your location, you'll have to decide how many storytelling props and puppets it makes sense to bring as well as whether you will bring items like shaky eggs or scarves. Then, you just have to account for someone being off-site for an hour or so once a month.

If you want to dip your toe in the water, I would recommend contacting your community center to see if it would like a program for families. The Beachwood Branch did this with the Jewish Community Center, and it offered a storytime right after a parent–child exercise class once a month. Both parties can then evaluate how it went and decide if it makes sense to be a regular offering. Another option would be to present a storytime at the community pool. You could talk to the pool staff about doing occasional storytimes throughout the summer during pool breaks.

Get creative and look for inexpensive ways to offer library programs and services within the community. By leaving the physical space of the library, you have a chance to connect with caregivers and kids and make them into regular library users.

Building Your Readers Advisory Toolbox

When looking for books for the infant to preschool age group, you should strive to add to your repertoire:

- A minimum of two board books each month
- A minimum of three picture books each month
- A minimum of five concept books a year
- A minimum of three nursery rhyme or Mother Goose books a year

---

References

Article

Milliot, Jim. "Print Sales Up Again in 2017." *Publishers Weekly* 265, no. 2 (January 8, 2018): 4.

Book

Wells, Rosemary. **Read to Your Bunny.** New York, NY: Scholastic Inc., 1999 (1997). unpaged. $3.99pa. 9780439087179pa.

Interviews

Beleske, Nicole Joy, and Becky Moldover. In interview with the author. May 22, 2018.
Harant, Andrew, and Liza Kahoe Arthur. In interview with the author. August 25, 2018.

Websites

Cedar Mill Community Libraries, Early Literacy. Accessed: October 28, 2017. http://library.cedarmill.org/kids/early-literacy/.
Every Child Ready to Read. Accessed: August 29, 2018. http://everychildready toread.org.

CHAPTER TWO

Apps, Blocks, Cartoons . . . What Is a Parent to Do?

Literacy is not just about learning to read. An equally important piece is the social and emotional development of children. Children who have a chance to play every day will learn many life skills that will help them later, including when they start learning to read. When parents become a part of play time, a strong bond develops between parents and the child. Through play children will learn skills such as sharing, taking turns, and following directions. They will practice fine and gross motor skills and exercise their imagination.

Play in the Library

Cuyahoga County Public Library made supporting parent-and-child play a focus for youth staff in 2017. Staff were trained to interact with families and model how to play with a child. The goal was not to tell caregivers what they were doing wrong. Rather staff were asked to offer more opportunities for play to happen at the library. This can involve getting down on the floor to play with kids using floor toys in the Children's Room as not all caregivers are comfortable doing this. If their parents did not play with them in this way, they may not realize they should be doing it with their own kids. Our interaction can be as simple as talking with parents about how doll houses and train tables inspire imaginative play. We can also help caregivers realize the importance of letting their kids take the lead on how play happens rather than direct it—but that they should still be a part of it.

Some other, nonthreatening ways to bring play into the library is to offer toys for play at the end of your storytimes. Having special toys that you bring out each week will give parents a reason to hang out a little longer at the library. When I have done this, play usually lasts about half an hour. Parents see other parents playing with their kids, and kids have a chance to practice sharing and taking turns with their peers.

Toys at the Library

Cuyahoga County Public Library's Toy Library celebrated 25 years of making toys available to library customers in 2018. The original Toy Library was housed in the Brooklyn Branch, and customers had to come directly to the branch to check out and return toys. In the late 2000s, Cuyahoga County made the decision to expand the Toy Library to all branches and close the service point at the Brooklyn Branch. The toys are now housed at the library's Administrative Offices, and families can request the toys for pickup at the branch of their choice. When toys are returned, they are always cleaned and sanitized at the Administrative Offices before another family can check them out.

As of 2018, there are over 1,000 toys circulating for ages zero through eight. Sue Kirschner, the literacy and outreach manager, is responsible for selecting these toys for customer use. She also selects toys for branch programming and floor toys for play in the library. The types of toys that Kirschner looks for fall into 12 categories.

- Active play
- Baby/toddler
- Blocks
- Games
- Learning skills
- Literacy
- Math
- Music
- Pretend play
- Puppets
- Puzzles
- Science and nature

From these categories, she orders toys such as soft dolls and puppets as well as play food and musical instruments to support imaginative play. Toys that support literacy as well as play include items such as alphabet-sequencing puzzles. Pull toys encourage movement and nesting cups involve basic problem-solving skills. When selecting toys for the toy library and branch use, Kirschner tends to stay away from toys that need batteries to function.

If you are looking to add toys to your branch for using after storytime, for Children's Room play, or for circulating, you will want to purchase toys from companies and manufactures that make high-quality toys. Kirschner has about two dozen sources that she likes to order toys from. Her top companies include Becker's School Supplies, Constructive Playthings, Fat Brain Toys, Kaplan, and Lakeshore. Manufactures that she trusts are Battat, HABA, Learning Resources, Petit Collage, and WePlay. The toys purchased from these sources hold up to heavy use from lots of kids and families playing.

Technology in the Library

Technology in libraries is not something new. Libraries have had computers for decades. They have offered VHS tapes and DVDs for customers to enjoy in the comfort of their own home. Some libraries even offer video games for play inside the library or at home. Nothing is wrong with expanding services beyond the book. In fact, libraries offering the most current forms of technology help narrow the digital divide and provide access to families that would otherwise not have it. However, there is also a responsibility for libraries to have a basic understanding of how these forms of technology can be used most effectively with kids and when it is best to not use or severely limit use. Specific areas that librarians can focus on are the amount of screen time that is recommended for kids and the best materials to view during that limited viewing time.

Screen Time

How much time children, especially kids who have not started kindergarten, spend viewing screens has been called into question for a long time. It used to be more focused on television watching and usually amounted to cartoons like Sesame Street or Care Bears. In the past decade, that conversation has shifted to include digital content. In October 2016, the Academy of American Pediatrics updated its recommendations for using technology with children. Not surprising to youth librarians, the recommendations stated that human interactions were the best ways to support children below two years (Media and Young Minds 2016). It translates to mean that playing with toys and listening to physical books read by caregivers will make greater connections in the brain and keep them on target developmentally. After age two, a limited amount of screen time with kids is recommended and that time is still best spent with parents experiencing the technology alongside their child.

App Use

Parents are challenged with choosing appropriate apps to share with their children and how much time they should let their children spend with a device or computer. Libraries do not want to shame parents or caregivers when it comes to using digital technology with their children at any age. Instead, we can mention reports like "Media and Youth Minds" in storytime as a form of guidance.

Taking it a step further, Stephanie C. Prato, the head of children's services at Simsbury Public Library in Simsbury, Connecticut, leads a team of youth staff who are adding app advisory to their normal readers advisory repertoire. The hope is that parents will come to think of the staff as technology experts like they are considered book experts.

Prato believes this is a natural extension of the services the library has offered in the past. Simsbury Public Library provides custom reading lists and suggestions for parents, and now they do the same thing for apps. With a little information from caregivers like the age of the child and the knowledge of a few areas of interest, an apps list is customized for the family. This type of transaction usually takes place at the service desk in the Children's Room but could also be a library service offered through e-mail.

Providing app recommendations is a great way to connect with and remove some stress for overwhelmed parents. Not only is it a challenge to search and find good apps, but it can be expensive to buy apps without being able to try them first. Having a literacy expert review apps can make parents feel confident that the time they spend playing an app with their child will not be marred by unexpected ads or poor app design. This is more common in free apps but can also happen with apps that families have purchased.

Librarians help their caregiver customers become content selectors of digital media just like they do with books and DVDs. When training her staff to provide app advisory, Prato reminds them that they recommend books and movies they might not have read or watched but they may have read reviews or heard about from a colleague. Websites that Prato uses to find reviews on apps include the following:

- ALA Best Apps for Teaching and Learning
- Teachers with Apps

She also recommends that if you are going to use an app in a program, it is always best to try it out yourself first. Just like with books, what a review says and what your experience is can be different. Try first so there are no surprises later.

Personalized recommendations for caregivers are wonderful, but depending on how crunched for time a family is or how busy the service desk might be, the one-on-one experience is not possible every time. In these cases, it is important to have printed handouts or bookmarks that list apps you think are the best of the best. It ensures that they will not leave empty-handed.

iPads in the Library

Another way for caregivers to test out new apps before buying can be found in the Children's Department at Simsbury. A group of eight locked-down iPads are available for families to use in the library. The settings are designed so that kids cannot access the Internet unless it is an approved website like Disney. Children and adults cannot add or delete content.

Simsbury Public Library does not set a limit for how long a child can use an iPad but instead leaves it up to the individual adult. This seems to work well with customers. Prato has witnessed caregivers letting kids play for five minutes and then they need to choose a book to read. Other caregivers set some kind of time limit up front, and some do not limit their child's play.

Building an App Collection

When you start to build your app collection, you will want to set aside a budget for purchasing new apps. Prato spends about $100 a year on apps, but this will depend on the number of iPads you are purchasing apps for. She assesses and updates the apps quarterly, or if it is a busy year, it might happen only twice a year. Along with the eight used in the Children's Department, an additional six iPads are used for library programs.

If your budget is tight already, especially if you just funded getting iPads in your library, you may have to rely on free apps for a while. This is okay but it is limiting in the long run. To find some extra dollars you can take a look at how other alternate formats in your library are performing. If one format, for example, music CDs, is not circulating as strongly as it used to, you could reallocate some funds to create an app budget. This is a good tip for any time you are adding a new format to the collection that does not come with grant money or additional funding attached.

When you're suggesting apps to families, the same logic applies of not limiting all the apps to free ones. Throwing in a few that require spending a dollar or three still keeps the cost down but might enhance the quality of the app experience at home.

Collection Development and Merchandising: Play

Recommending books that encourage movement and interaction to care-givers will make family reading time lots of fun. Consider putting up a display of play-related books near the space you place your toys. It can lead to natural recommendations from library staff as you witness imaginative play.

Play titles, especially ones that have flaps, tabs, or other moveable parts, will show their wear pretty quickly, so make sure you look inside before you add to your display. Beware of small pieces and parts in these books. I had to recall a *Pat the Bunny* version that had a rattle piece between the pages that could cause choking if the pages were torn. A similar instance also happened with *The Pout-Pout Fish Halloween Faces*. This time there were google eyes on the last page that poked through each dye-cut page. The books were removed because if the eyes got loose they could also be choking hazards for little ones. Play should be fun but also safe. If you're not sure about the size of a piece in a book, you can try a choke tube or a paper-towel tube in a pinch. No matter what, error on the side of caution.

Books for Play and Quiet Time

The more books that are shared with a child, the better the child's vocabulary will be, but also the better developed the creativity of the child will be. Incorporating books and reading into play time and relaxation time helps to reinforce that reading is fun family time. Here are some great books to use for library program planning and to share with parents for at-home reading time.

Active Stories

In a library program, we model asking kids questions about what is happening and will even offer activities to extend books. Both the questions and activities are best if they are ones that parents can re-create at home. These books tend to be the type used in storytime. They get kids shouting out the reframe or curious about what the texture of a page will feel like.

Brantley-Newton, Vanessa. **Grandma's Purse.** New York, NY: Alfred Al Knopf, 2018. unpaged. $17.99. 9781524714314.
    A purse is a wonderful treasure trove of trinkets to be discovered by little ones. Read this one and then explore a purse together talking about what you find. (Picture Book)
Joosse, Barbara M., and Anneke Lisberg. **Better Together: A Book of Family.** Illustrated by Jared Andrew Schorr. New York, NY: Abrams Appleseed, 2017. unpaged. $14.95. 9781419725388.
    Foldout pages and die cuts make the telling of the story a little more fun. (Picture Book)

Laden, Nina. **Peek-a Moo!** San Francisco, CA: Chronicle Books LLC, 2017. unpaged. $6.99. 978145214749.
> The die cuts hint at what is going to happen on the next page. An added bonus is that it also encourages a game of peek-a-boo between the parent and the child. (Board Book)

Lin, Grace. **A Big Mooncake for Little Star.** New York, NY: Little, Brown and Company, 2018. unpaged. $17.99. 9780316404488.
> Little Star just can't leave the yummy mooncake alone. Cooking is an active hobby that adults and children can enjoy together. (Picture Book)

Little Bee Books. **Animal Shapes: A Touch-and-Feel Book.** New York, NY: Little Bee Books, 2015. unpaged. $6.99. 9781499800395.
> A great choice for kids who like a tactile book to help keep them involved in the story. A fun extension for parents would be to gather items up around the house and then have their child touch to see how different things feel. (Board Book)

Litwin, Eric. **If You're Groovy and You Know It, Hug a Friend.** Illustrated by Tom Lichtenheld. New York, NY: Orchard Books, 2018. unpaged. (Groovy Joe). $9.99. 9780545883801.
> Sing and act out this twist on the traditional "If You're Happy and You Know It" song. (Picture Book)

Matheson, Christie. **Plant the Tiny Seed.** New York, NY: Greenwillow Books, 2017. unpaged. $15.99. 9780062393395.
> By following the instructions provided by the text, kids will help to plant and grow a seed. This book helps develop a natural back and forth between the adult and the child. Parents can then have their child plant seeds in a small pot or help in the flower beds or garden at home. (Picture Book)

Mitton, Tony. **Dinosaurumpus!** Illustrated by Guy Parker-Rees. New York, NY: Cartwheel Books, 2017 (2002). unpaged. (Story Play). $5.99. 9781338115369.
> After reading about the dinosaurs finding their dancing groove, caregivers are given tips for extension activities like creating their own memory game or dance. Each book in the Story Play series offers similar opportunities. (Picture Book)

Sirett, Dawn. **Baby Dinosaurs.** Illustrated by Peter Minister and Charlotte Milner. New York, NY: DK Publishing, 2017. unpaged. (Follow the Trail). $9.99. 9781465456694.
> The Follow the Trail series helps kids practice tracing with their finger. This fine motor skill is a precursor to tracing letters before learning to write them. Kids can practice their scribbling with a crayon on a piece of white paper. (Board Book)

Thompkins-Bigelow, Jamilah. **Mommy's Khimar.** Illustrated by Ebony Glenn. New York, NY: Salaam Reads, 2018. unpaged. $17.99. 9781534400597.
> Dress-up is an activity that all children like to play. In this story, a Muslim girl plays dress-up with her mom's head scarves. (Picture Book)

Wright, Kenneth. **Lola Dutch.** Illustrated by Sarah Jane Wright. New York, NY: Bloomsbury, 2018. unpaged. $17.99. (Lola Dutch). 9781681195513.
A unique packaging for a picture book. The inside cover is a doll house and paper dolls are on the flap. This book can be enjoyed simply as a story but it is also a wonderful opportunity to do a show and tell with parents who might want to buy a copy for their home library. There are great chances for imaginative play to be found in this book. (Picture Book)

Relaxation Stories

Gayle Schreiber was an educator for over 30 years. She has practiced yoga for over 40 years and tai chi for 7 years. Her experience in teaching made her aware of the importance of helping kids feel calm and in control. In 2018, she became certified by Angel Bear Yoga and Tai Chi for Kids so that she could share the benefits of these practices in schools. She does recommend that you be familiar with yoga or tai chi before taking an online course.

Benefits of Yoga, Tai Chi, and Mindfulness

- Enhance physical flexibility
- Support balance and coordination
- Manage stress through breathing and healthy movement
- Build concentration, listening and literacy skills
- Boost self-esteem and confidence
- Build empathy toward self and others
- Develop imagination (Schreiber, G. 2018)

To help kids play their tai chi, yoga, and mindfulness, here are some excellent resources for both librarians and caregivers to introduce them to the practices.

Bersma, Danielle, and Marjoke Visscher. **Yoga Games for Children: Fun and Fitness with Postures, Movements, and Breath.** Translated Amina Marix Evans. Illustrated by Alex Kooistra. Alameda, CA: A Hunter House SmartFun Book, 2003 (1994). 146p. $14.95pa. 9780897933896pa.
With over 60 games to choose from, there is something for all fitness and age levels. Two great activities are 42 and 43. They help kids recognize how anger and happiness feel and how to deal with these emotions. (Reference Book)

Chopra, Mallika. **Just Breathe: Meditation, Mindfulness, Movement, and More.** Illustrated by Brenna Vaughan. Philadelphia, PA: RP Kids, 2018. 128p. $12.99pa. 9780762491582pa.
Teaches caregivers ways to help their children learn to calm themselves in their everyday environment and when they are stressed out. (Reference Book)

Gates, Mariam. **Good Night Yoga: A Pose-by-Pose Bedtime Story.** Illustrated by Sarah Jane Hinder. Boulder, CO: Sounds True, 2015. unpaged. $17.95. 9781622034666.

> The simple story takes kids through easy breathing and yoga poses to quiet them before going to bed. The author and illustrator also have a morning version and one for kids to do with a friend. (Picture Book, Nonfiction)

Gates, Mariam. **Meditate with Me: A Step-by-Step Mindfulness Journey.** Illustrated by Margarita Surnaite. New York, NY: Dial Books for Young Readers, 2017. unpaged. $17.99. 9780399186615.

> It breaks down how to meditate for young kids wanting to try. There is also a very simple craft project that helps demonstrate relaxed breathing. (Picture Book, Nonfiction)

Hinder, Sarah Jane. **Yoga Bear: Simple Animal Poses for Little Ones.** Boulder, CO: Sounds True, Inc., 2008. unpaged. $9.95. 9781683640752.

> A board book that incorporates diverse children and animals to teach simple yoga poses to toddlers. (Board Book)

Sileo, Frank J. PhD. **Bee Still: An Invitation to Meditation.** Illustrated by Claire Keay. Washington, DC: Magination Press, 2018. unpaged. $16.99. 9781433828706.

> A story explains to children what meditation is. The back matter offers parents additional tips for doing meditation with their children. (Picture Book)

Willey, Kira. **Breathe Like a Bear: 30 Mindful Moments for Kids to Feel Calm and Focused Anytime, Anywhere.** Illustrated by Anni Betts. Emmaus, PA: Rodale Kids, 2017. 84p. $14.99pa. 9781623368838pa.

> Interactive text walks listeners through ways to imagine, energize, and focus. (Reference Book)

Yoo, Taeeun. **You Are a Lion!: And Other Fun Yoga Poses.** New York, NY: Nancy Paulsen Books, 2012. unpaged. $17.99. 9780399256028.

> Follow the text, make a pose, and then turn the page to see what animal you are. (Picture Book)

Programs That Promote Family Play

Books and play can go hand and hand at the library. The two programs that follow merge literacy and play to provide families with unique program experiences.

Storybook Adventure—Cuyahoga County Public Library, Ohio, Berea Branch

If you are looking to do a splashy event that ties into books, play, and STEAM, then you need look no further. This program joins all these components together for a memorable, staff-led program that will bring in the community or unite the staff of a school.

Background

In 2017, Jennifer M. Winkler and the staff at the Berea Branch decided to host a grand storybook adventure program during the summer. The goal was to include STEAM and play into each station and center the stations around nursery rhymes, fairy tales, or folklore characters. This stemmed from Winkler noticing that many younger parents were not familiar with these characters or even sharing nursery rhymes with their children.

Planning

The program was hosted outdoors so it did involve working with the city to get permission to use the gazebo, pavilion, and woods that are adjacent to the library's parking lot. From there, the staff had to decide what the stations would be and how many volunteers would be needed to operate each one. Winkler felt strongly that it should be library staff who led each craft and who would be dressed up as the storybook characters. Teen volunteers could be extra character props like Little Bo Peep's sheep and volunteers could help with setup. The branch manager reached out to other branch managers for staff volunteers because the Berea Branch could not run the program and help other customers with just their own branch's staff.

If you don't have an outdoor space near your library, you could do this program inside. You will also need to plan for the possibility of rain and have an indoor option. You would just need to adjust the number of stations and activities to fit the space you have inside. If you work in a school, this would be a fantastic way to get the whole school involved or you could do it with a grade or two. What fun it would be to get teachers, parents, and even the principal to dress up, stay in character, and interact with the students.

Stations

The stations vary a little each year but here is what they looked like for 2018. Each one was a little different and touched on a different literacy or STEAM area but all encouraged play with everyday materials. The crafts were quick and easy for the kids to create.

Humpty Dumpty. Humpty Dumpty had been put back together but was now separated from "all the king's horses and all the king's men," so he needed the kids to get him over the wall that was keeping them apart.

The activity here was a catapult that would toss a papier-mâché egg over the wall. The kids and the parents were encouraged to discuss what action would be needed to get the egg up high enough and with enough force to actually make it over the wall.

Little Red Riding Hood. At this station, Little Red Riding Hood was tired from all her trips through the forest to Grandma's house and the Big Bad Wolf was on the loose again. So they had come up with a great way to beat the wolf and save Little Red some steps—a zipline.

There were two ziplines, one for the wolf and one for Little Red (aka the kids). This was done by stringing a clothesline at an angle. Then there were baskets and plastic play food that the kids could select from to build their baskets. They would run it along the zipline and see if it could outpace the Big Bad Wolf. Whether it did or not, it was a perfect chance for the staff to get the kids thinking about why they got the result they did. They could ask questions like: Was their basket too heavy or not heavy enough? Did the number of items in the basket or types of items factor in? This showed caregivers how to have critical thinking discussion with their kids when working with everyday materials.

A slight variation that was also used included cards that told the kids what types of items to place in the baskets. There were things like specific food so that they would be sending a balanced meal of all the food groups or simply adding something sweet to the rest of their choices. This was good for the older kids, but for younger, they might get a card that tells them to add a red- or purple-colored food to their basket.

Three Little Pigs. The premise for this station was that the oldest pig had kicked out pigs two and three because they were too messy. They now had to build their own houses, and they still needed to stand up to the breath of the Big Bad Wolf.

A spinner would determine if kids got straw, sticks, bricks, or a material of their choice. The straw was made from plastic straws (cut off the bendy part), sticks were popsicle sticks, and the bricks were foam bricks. Standing paper pigs were given to each child, and they had to build a home from their material that was taller than the pig. Once their structure was built, the Big Bad Wolf made an appearance. Two hairdryers were dressed up like wolves and used to blow the house down. If kids didn't want to use the hairdryers, they could use their own breath.

Creating houses involved using engineering skills. It also modeled for the parents how to have a dialogic conversation with their child. They could talk about how they were using the building materials, what they thought would happen once the Big Bad Wolf did his thing, and possibly most important, what they could do to make their structure stronger in the future. As kids really got into the activity, staff also talked about doing the same activity at home but maybe trying it with items like Legos. Again, the idea was that these activities could be done outside of the library and likely would not cost the family any money to replicate.

Alice in Wonderland. Alice was just back from Wonderland and wanted the kids to know what the experience was like for her. The character talked a little bit about how she ended up in Wonderland and even asked the kids if they had ever seen a white rabbit.

Then to have the kids experience what it was like in Wonderland, they created kaleidoscopes from paper tubes. This craft was a little more involved, and the staff created 200 craft kits. They actually ran out and plan to have 300 craft projects for kids in 2019. While the kids were creating their kaleidoscopes, it gave Winkler (Alice) a chance to talk to them about how the device actually works, including why they will not see the same image twice.

Literary Stations. Mary Mary Quite Contrary was at the library, which was the starting point. The activity here was creating a magical memory foam frame.

The Pied Pieper picked up the families at the Mary Mary station and brought them outside to the start of the Storybook Adventure that was denoted by a large book sign created by the staff. It had Storybook Adventure on it as well as the library's name. They wanted families to recognize the program was presented by the library and not the city.

Little Bo Beep was also near the entrance, and she would encourage families to move about the stations based on how busy they were rather than going in a particular order. She also told the kids to be on the lookout for her missing sheep and to call out "sheep go home" if they found them.

The Sing a Song of Sixpence Maid and Mother Goose shared nursery rhymes. The Maid played the nursery rhyme songs on the ukulele. Mother Goose gave out feathers to kids who could recite a nursery rhyme. For those who did not know one, she had a cube with rhyme images. Kids could roll the cube and then practice the rhyme they landed on with Mother Goose.

A pirate station had games for kids to play that helped with gross and fine motor skills as well as critical thinking. One example was a walk-the-plank activity.

In the woods, they also did additional vignettes from the various nursery rhymes. They did not identify which nursery rhyme they were from but, instead, allowed the families to discuss among themselves and decide. The staff were looking to foster conversation among the family members. Winkler said the families did not always guess the rhyme the library had picked, but they always had logical reasons for their choices.

Some examples of the vignettes included: at the bottom of a small hill there was a pail and a first-aid kit (Jack and Jill), a moon up in a tree (Hey

Diddle Diddle), and spilled curds and whey with tiny footprints walking away (Little Miss Muffet).

Books were on display at the library and families did journey back to check books out. Winkler would love to have a tent with books on display for check out as part of the Storybook Adventure outdoor space next year as she felt they would get even more families to take books home.

Advertising

They did include the program in the library's print guide as well as online. Other avenues for promoting the program came during storytimes and other library programs throughout the summer. They also asked the schools and preschools to share in their monthly newsletters. Finally, the library's marketing department mentioned it on Facebook the day before the program and then they posted short videos of the actual program while it was happening.

Attendance

The first year saw 275 people attend and in 2018 there were over 500. Many had planned to attend because they had heard about the program in advance. They also found families that were either driving by or had come to the library for other reasons were joining in.

A couple of memorable comments were made by attendees including those who missed the witch from Hansel and Gretel who performed the year before. The other was when people would ask where they got their presenters because they wanted to book them for their child's birthday party. The caregivers were surprised to learn that the staff were all library workers.

Parent Participation

Parents and other caring adults were part of each activity and discussion. Mostly they saw families but a daycare also attended. The library did require that kids be accompanied by a caring adult. The staff members incorporated ideas for modifying at home and shared these tips with parents at each station as the kids worked on the project. They wanted to show the parents that having fun and learning did not have to mirror school. It should be "early literacy entertainment" and playful in nature (Winkler 2018).

Public Library. An exciting piece of offering this program is that it brings in people who are not regular library users. These families who had such a fun time would then ask about other library storytimes and programs because they were planning to come back. A huge win for getting foot traffic into your building.

School Library. The win here would be getting teachers and parents involved so they can see all the great things you offer in the library space. You show your value as a partner and resource for other lessons the teachers in the building might be looking to try out.

Yoga Play—Akron Summit County Public Library, Ohio, Main Library

Using knowledge from a personal hobby can enrich the work that you do at your library and provide unique play and learning opportunities for families. Kimberly Alberts and Anne-Marie Savoie, children's librarians, did just that when they started offering yoga programs at the library. Both have been practicing yoga for about 15 years and have offered programs in a library setting for three years.

Background

When Alberts joined the Main Library staff at Akron Summit County Public Library, she had already done some yoga programming at her previous library. Savoie had an established Yoga Play program at Main Library but her co-presenter had just retired. The two staff members joined together to create a Yoga Play program that meshes both of their experiences.

What It's All About

Yoga Play is offered once a quarter as a month-long series. The Main Library offers yoga on Monday mornings for ages three to five and caregivers. They have found that day and time works best for their community. Each week has a theme and they plan the program around it. The week I observed, they did a Park theme. The program is a mix of traditional yoga poses and creative movement that is modified for a preschool audience. Each child gets a yoga mat and caregivers are encouraged to take a mat and participate too.

Room Setup

Alberts and Savoie set the room up in a circle. They are seated as part of the circle, and the yoga mats fan out around them to form the rest of the circle. Savoie likes to use found items from around the house, library, and nature to set the stage for the day's theme. Cardboard was used to create a tree for a park setting. Stuffed animals and flowers helped authenticate the space the week I attended.

Access to a sound system is needed for playing songs. Other props might include bean bags for a breathing buddy or homemade stars like Akron uses.

The stars are about 8 inches in diameter. Made from cardboard, they have a bean bag attached to the center of the star and then the cardboard and bean bag are covered in shiny silver wrap.

Additional set up is done for the free play that happens after the program. This will depend on the crafts you choose to do. Alberts and Savoie recommend creating play from things found around the house. They want to hear caregivers saying, "We could do this at home."

The Program

As families come in and gather on the yoga mats, they are encouraged to remove their shoes and socks. Albert and Savoie do the same. Soft, instrumental music is playing in the background to help set the mood. The area right behind the leaders is set for the theme but everything used can be touched and moved by the kids who like to wander and explore.

They start with an opening hello song "Namaste" and the use of a chime with a hammer. Everyone sings: "Namaste KID'S NAME, Namaste KID'S NAME, Namaste KID'S NAME, it's time to do yoga." After their name is sung, the child gets to tap the chime and then everyone listens until the sound stops. Savoie lets the families know they are waking up their ears with this exercise. Next, they move into breathing and proper posture that is led by Alberts. She uses an expanding and contracting ball to highlight how to breathe in and out as you move through yoga poses. She also demonstrates how to sit up straight for good posture.

Alberts and Savoie will then alternate explaining 6 to 10 yoga poses and movements for kids to try. Parents can do them alongside or help their child if they need it. Poses like tree, dog, and table will be interspersed with creative movements like cricket and flower. For the Park theme, the table pose was used to pretend they were having a picnic and Albert and Savoie placed plastic food on the kids backs. They had to keep their backs flat in order to keep the food from falling off.

A story is read and a song is sung related to the theme. Then they will move to rest time. Here each child gets a shiny star, bean bag, or even a beanie baby to act as their breathing buddy. The kids and adults lie down on their yoga mats with their breathing buddy on their stomach. A towel or blanket is also given to the kids to make it cozy. Savoie demonstrates for the families, while Alberts turns on and off the soft instrumental music. Alberts tries to get the kids to be still for two to two and half minutes. Some weeks this works better than others but Alberts stresses not giving up. Kids have good and bad weeks, but it is good for kids to practice calming themselves and a great exercise for caregivers to incorporate at home. The formal program ends with an affirmation. Kids say, "I am Smart," and touch their heads; then say, "I am Loved," and touch their hearts; and then say, "I am Wonderful" and reach their arms out to their sides. This is repeated a couple of times.

Free play and activities come next. The activities are set up by Albert and Savoie as the kids put their shoes and socks back on, help roll up the yoga mats, and enjoy a small bottle of water provided by the library. As the children play, Albert and Savoie model interactive play between adults and children. They help parents engage in a dialogue with their children while they play.

Activity: Paint the Branch. A large branch from Alberts's yard is placed on a tarp. Kids are given foam brushes and their choice of paint. They then add color to the branch in their own artistic way.

Activity: Garden Soup. A couple of large bowls of water, some plastic ladles or spoons, fresh flowers, and scissors are placed on a low table. Kids have the chance to practice holding scissors and cutting as they select flowers for the garden soup.

Activity: Potting Soil. A sensory experience is created with plastic tubs full of potting soil. Kids can dig and touch the soil using sand box tools and plastic spoons.

Activity: Outdoor Play Inside. Hula hoops and a kid's basketball hoop round out the activities. These activities help with coordination skills.

No Experience at Yoga

If you do not already practice yoga, you will need to do a little homework before diving in. Alberts suggests taking some basic yoga classes. By doing this you will observe how a yoga class flows from start to finish. You will learn more about the importance of breathing and how to move with the breath.

Yoga Training. Savoie also recommends looking for a training class like she took from Childlight Yoga. It was a weekend long class that focused on yoga poses and games for a child audience.

Professional Resources. When Alberts was researching yoga programs, she came across these three resources. They are great for learning poses that are simplified for using with children as well as ideas for using them in a library setting.

Flynn, Lisa. **Yoga for Children: 200+ Yoga Poses, Breathing Exercises, and Meditations for Healthier, Happier, More Resilient Children.** Avon, MA: Adams Media, 2013. 319p. $17.95pa. 9781440554636pa.

Rawlinson, Adrienne. **Creative Yoga for Children: Inspiring the Whole Child Through Yoga, Songs, Literature, and Games: Forty Fun, Ready-to-Teach Lessons for Ages Four through Twelve.** Berkeley, CA: North Atlantic Books, 2013. 208p. $16.95pa. 9781583945544pa.

Scherrer, Katie. **Stories, Songs, and Stretches!: Creating Playful Storytimes with Yoga and Movement.** Chicago, IL: ALA Editions, 2017. 100p. $48.00pa. 9780838915448pa.

Why You Should Try It

Yoga Play is the perfect opportunity to teach caregivers how to play, be silly, and have fun with their children if it does not come naturally. It also shows both the parent and the child how to relax through quiet breathing periods. You do not have to be an expert to offer a yoga program in your library. In fact, Alberts feels that it is actually less intimidating for parents if you are a novice as well.

Trying It at Your Library

Yoga programs can work at both school and public libraries. The program that Akron does is structured for about 45 minutes of yoga poses and breathing and 30 minutes for play. It is led by two staff members who plan and present together. The entire program is like a conversation between librarians and kids, with caregivers listening in.

Usually it also includes about 30 minutes before and after to set up and clean up. Depending on your room size and the amount of time you can devote, you could shorten the time to 30 minutes of yoga and 30 minutes of play. The other option would just be yoga poses and breathing for 30 minutes. This would cut down on your setup and cleanup time too.

Public Library. If you would like to offer a yoga program, you will need to find a person or two who has experience or is willing to go through training. A Childlight Yoga weekend session can run around $450 for the class. Then you will need to take the steps to determine a good day and time and how long the program will last. You will also need to decide whether you will include play. While Akron focuses on the preschool age group, yoga programs and play can work with any age group.

School Library. If you have yoga experience or are willing to get some training, you can offer yoga programs at your school. It might be as simple as teaching kids some breathing techniques to calm themselves before or during a test. You can also carry books in the library on yoga, meditation, and breathing for kids to check out. Taking care of mind and body helps kids be better able to learn.

Building Your Readers Advisory Toolbox

Start adding books and media that are playful, silly, and promote mindfulness to your cache.

- Read at least one picture book or board book a month that can be extended to incorporate play.
- Read at least one picture book a quarter that relates to yoga, meditation, or relaxation for children.
- Play with one new app a month.

References

Article

"Media and Young Minds." *Pediatrics* 138, no. 5 (2016). doi:10.1542/peds .2016-2591.

Books

Diesen, Deborah. **The Pout-Pout Fish Halloween Faces.** Illustrated by Dan Hanna. New York, NY: Farrar Straus Giroux Books for Young Readers, 2018. $9.99. 9780374304508.

Kunhardt, Dorothy. **Pat the Bunny.** New York, NY: Golden Books, an imprint of Random House Children's Books, 2011 (1940). unpaged. $14.99. 978030 7200471.

Interviews

Alberts, Kimberly, and Anne-Marie Savoie. In interview with the author. September 5, 2018.

Prato, Stephanie C. In phone interview with the author. August 3, 2018.

Schreiber, Gayle. In interview with the author. September 25, 2018.

Winkler, Jennifer M. In interview with the author. August 3, 2018.

Websites

ALA Best Apps for Teaching and Learning. Accessed September 18, 2018. http:// www.ala.org/aasl/standards/best/apps.

Angel Bear Yoga. Accessed September 30, 2018. http://www.angelbearyoga.com.

Battat. Accessed September 30, 2018. http://www.battatco.com/collections/my-btoys.

Becker's School Supplies. Accessed September 30, 2018. https://www.shopbecker.com.

Childlight Yoga. Accessed September 5, 2018. http://childlightyoga.com.

Constructive Playthings. Accessed September 30, 2018. https://constructiveplaythings.com.

Fat Brain Toys. Accessed September 30, 2018. https://constructiveplaythings.com.

HABA. Accessed September 30, 2018. https://www.habausa.com.

Kaplan. Accessed September 30, 2018. https://www.kaplanco.com.

Lakeshore. Accessed September 30, 2018. https://www.lakeshorelearning.com.

Learning Resources. Accessed September 30, 2018. https://www.learningresources.com.

Petit Collage. Accessed September 30, 2018. https://petitcollage.com.

Tai Chi for Kids. Accessed September 30, 2018. https://www.taichiforkids.com.

Teachers with Apps. Accessed September 18, 2018. https://www.teacherswithapps.com.

"Toys and Bookable Kits." Cuyahoga County Public Library. Accessed September 30, 2018. https://www.cuyahogalibrary.org/Borrow/Toys-and-Bookable-Kits.aspx.

WePlay. Accessed September 30, 2018. http://www.weplay.com.tw.

How Do I Teach My Child to Read?

In 2011, I had the honor of reading for the 2012 Theodor Seuss Geisel Award, which is administered annually by the Association of Library Service to Children. The charge of this committee is to find "the most distinguished American book for beginning readers published in English in the United States during the preceding year" (Welcome to the [Theodor Seuss] Geisel Award home page! 2018). During my year of reading books for beginning readers, I learned a lot about what kids need in order to have a good experience with the book they are holding in their hands.

With the creation of the Geisel Award, publishers stepped up the layouts and storytelling of beginning reader titles. These high-quality books are just what librarians and caregivers are looking for. The stories and art capture children's imaginations and encourage them to learn the individual words in order to be able to read a book on their own. It is a journey that families embark on together when the time is right.

When to Start

Nothing is more magical in my mind than when a child starts down the path to becoming a reader. This path really begins at birth when parents start reading to their baby every day. Then usually sometime between the ages of five and six, the vocabulary heard and the letters learned start to become familiar words on the page. A child can read a word or two and then, overtime, a sentence and then, over even more time, a paragraph. This does not happen overnight and can be a daunting task for parents who want to send their child to kindergarten reading.

Type A parents may start this process at the young end of the spectrum, as early as two years old, and some parents will start to panic a little by the end of kindergarten if their child is not reading. If parents are looking for a sign that their child is ready to start learning to read more formally, they can look at how their child interacts with books.

- Is the child memorizing the stories heard repeatedly?
- Is the child trying to read the words on the page to help tell the story?
- Is the child excited about learning to read?

If the answers to these questions are "yes," then the child is likely ready to start learning to read. This can mean that the child is at the stage of learning the letters and their sounds, the stage of putting the letters and sounds together to make words, or the stage of being able to start recognizing words on the page. Learning to read happens in stages, and each one is important to the process.

Ideally, children's and school librarians will work with the parent and the child to find books that are on an appealing subject and that start with few words on the page and lots of large illustrations and build to more challenging sentence structure over time. Unfortunately, it is not always that simple. Once the word *level* is added to the conversation, learning to read can become more number or letter focused rather than individual kid and interest focused.

The Challenges of Leveling Books

One of the biggest areas of support librarians can offer is helping caregivers navigate the leveling world. With their first child, parents will probably be flummoxed about what the numbers or letters mean and will need a translator to assist them in helping select books for their child. Working with levels is not the way most librarians like to make recommendations, but we realize it comes with the territory. So, let us break it down between leveling systems used by schools and those used by publishers.

Leveling Systems

Leveling of books is usually related to Accelerated Reader (AR), Lexile, Fountas and Pinnell, or other guided reading levels. These are guidelines that many school districts use to evaluate a student's reading progress. Assigning specific levels to read is done in an attempt to find just the right reading level for each child—a level that challenges the child but is not too difficult and, therefore, discouraging. This sounds good, and when communicated to parents, it can seem like a terrific idea. How simple it seems to just look for a level rather than look at the books themselves to determine the right fit. The problem is that assigning a specific level to a child severely limits what the child has access to read. The interest of a child is left out of the equation, and many times, so is appropriateness of the text.

School Library Perspective

Jessica Gillis is a school librarian at John M. Tobin Montessori School, a public school in Cambridge, Massachusetts. Her school library serves kids in preschool through fifth grade. The school uses Fountas & Pinnell to assess the children, but she does not use this system in her library. She does pull out and shelve her easy readers as well as chapter book series for emerging readers separately. Occasionally, she will check what a child's letter level is to get a better idea for what types of books to recommend, but she does not look up that letter for a list of books to suggest. It just gives her an idea where the child is as a reader, and then she uses her professional knowledge to pull books for that reader.

Pressure from teachers, administrators, and parents to make finding leveled books super easy with labels on the books and shelving standards that throw out the Dewey Decimal system in favor of levels are challenges school librarians may contend with. If you find yourself in this type of situation, I would start by explaining that leveling systems were never intended to be used to make book recommendation directly to children.

The creators of the Fountas and Pinnell system are adamant that their system should not be used to limit a child's choice of books, which happens when children are not allowed to read outside their level. In fact, they "designed the F&P Text Level Gradient™ to help teachers think more analytically about the characteristics of texts and their demands on the reading process, and the A to Z levels were used to show small steps from easiest to most difficult" (Parrott 2017). The idea was that teachers could use this information to help them prepare lessons but not as a system to brand kids.

Public Library Perspective

It can be a little easier to stay away from shelving by a particular system in a public library. When I get asked about shelving by AR, I explain that each school had to purchase tests, and so the books a student could read and then find a test on at each school were different. There was no way around having to look up titles on the printed lists. Most caregivers got it but were still frustrated by the time spent hunting for that perfect 2.5 book.

The compromise Cuyahoga County Public Library made several years ago was to import the AR and Lexile levels in through our integrated library system, Innovative Interfaces Inc. Now when customers and staff look up titles in the Encore catalog, they can also check specific levels. This keeps labels off books but still allows families to find the information if they need it. It also protects the privacy of the reader because it makes it less clear which books are above or below grade level.

Publisher Levels

If things were not complicated enough, you also need to be aware of the leveling systems used by publishers. Many times, these leveling systems will be numerical with a level 1 or level 2 on the spine or cover of the book. Sometimes it will be a letter. The challenge here is that the levels and letters do not always correspond to leveling systems like AR or Lexile, and they do not mean the same thing from publisher to publisher. This is confusing enough for librarians, but it is paralyzing for caregivers.

Parents are trying their best to make reading fun and not too hard, but selecting the right book can feel impossible. It is time-consuming and leaves parents feeling aggravated. Librarians, both school and public, need to be current on the beginning reader books that are in their collection so they can make the recommendations that cut through the leveling red tape.

Collection Development and Merchandising: From Pre-Reader to Reader

When kids start learning to read, they have lots of choices as there are tons of books published each year that are made specifically for this process. With the wide variety available, there truly is something for every reader. Because there are so many and they are written for the different stages of a reader, the help of a librarian is necessary to find the best choices.

Beginning Readers

One area of the collection I have always found to circulate extremely well is the beginning reader section. When I do a slow-moving list for items that have not circulated in the past year, there are only a handful, and the few that are listed tend to end up being missing. Because they circulate at such a great rate, other actions need to be taken to make sure items are weeded out as they get worn out. Instead of a slow-moving list, you might want to do an aged report for items over 10 years old or for items that have circulated 20 times or more. You do not have to weed everything on the list, but you will want to use your professional judgment on whether to keep, replace, or withdraw to make room for new titles.

It is so important to capture the interest of kids as they start down the path to reading success. If at all possible, shelve the first readers on lower shelves so that a kindergartener or a second grader can reach the books to browse for something to read. While you want a caregiver to be there to help in the decision-making process, it is hard for children to take ownership if they cannot reach the books.

Leveled Series

This list of level readers and their publishers is not meant to include every one available but, instead, offer you a variety of examples of good titles and publishers to look out for.

Capstone Publishing—Stone Arch Readers
Crow, Melinda Melton. **Brave Fire Truck.** Illustrated by Chad Thompson. Mankato, MN: Stone Arch Books, 2012. 31p. $22.65. 9781434230294.
A level-one book that has only a few words per page and lots of the words are repeated throughout. A great choice for kids just starting the learning-to-read process. While not as flashy as some of the other series listed, these early readers are spot on for using limited vocabulary.

HarperCollins—I Can Read
Garton, Sam. **Let's Go Swimming!** New York, NY: Balzer + Bray, 2017. 32p. (Otter). $16.99. 9780062366641.
HarperCollins uses the level My First Shared Reading for kids in the pre-reading stage. When reading the Otter series, caregivers may still be doing the majority of the reading aloud, but the layout is conducive to young eyes and the repetition will help listeners start to recognize words on the page as they work up to joining in the storytelling fun.

Holiday House—I Like to Read
Long, Ethan. **Dance, Dance, Dance!** New York, NY: Holiday House, 2018. unpaged. $14.95. 9780823438594.
The line-up of authors and illustrators writing the I Like to Read series are some of the best in the business. The layout of the book depends on the talent creating the work but each is well thought out. In this particular story, there is a lot of repetition and the layout has more of a comic book style using word bubbles for the narrative.

Houghton Mifflin Harcourt—Green Light Readers
Nolen, Jerdine. **Block Party Surprise.** Illustrated by Michelle Henninger. Boston, MA: Houghton Mifflin Harcourt, 2015. 41p. (Bradford Street Buddies). $12.99. 9780544358621.

With multiple sentences on each page, this level-three reader is for kids who are ready to read independently according to the Green Light Reader system.

Lee & Low Books—Dive into Reading

Hooks, Gwendolyn. **Music Time.** Illustrated by Shirley Ng-Benitez. New York, NY: Lee & Low Books Inc., 2017. 32p. $14.95. 9781620143438.

Lee & Low has their own leveling system that includes: Early Emergent, Emergent, Early Fluent, and Fluent. This Emergent title includes chapters that each tells a piece of the overarching plot but each chapter has a clear ending. Writing this way allows a reader to enjoy a book in chunks.

Little Brown and Company—Passport to Reading

Christopher, Matt. **The Dog That Pitched a No-Hitter.** Illustrated by Steve Bjorkman. New York, NY: Little Brown and Company, 2013 (1988). 48p. $3.99pa. 9780316218481pa.

The dialogue, short paragraphs, and plot that carries from chapter to chapter offer a level-three book that is just right for kids reading independently but not quite ready for a longer chapter book.

Macmillan—My Readers

Griffiths, Andy. **The Cat, the Rat, and the Baseball Bat.** Illustrated by Terry Denton. New York, NY: Square Fish, 2013. 32p. $15.99. 9781250027733.

Rhyming words and word families are used to tell a nonsense story. The limited and purposeful vocabulary and the illustrations of new and classic characters will help readers build confidence as they read.

Penguin Books—Penguin Young Readers

Adler, David A. **Don't Throw It to Mo!** Illustrated by Sam Ricks. New York, NY: Penguin Young Readers, 2015. 32p. (Mo). $14.99. 9780670016310.

This series under the Penguin umbrella provides African American kids a regular kid who looks like them, and each book tackles a different sport. These books are just right for kids ready to move beyond works with a more controlled vocabulary and word count. The books in the Penguin Young Readers line use guided reading levels.

Random House Books for Young Readers—Step into Reading

Liberts, Jennifer. **Go, Go, Trucks!** Illustrated by Mike Yamada. New York, NY: Random House, 2017. 32p. $12.99. 9780399549526.

Repetition and rhythm will help beginning readers work on fluency as they read. Colorful illustrations will assist kids in deciphering unfamiliar words. This is a step-one book that is truly meant for someone just learning to read.

Rodale Kids—Curious Readers

Capozzi, Suzy. **I Am Strong.** Illustrated by Eren Unten. New York, NY: Rodale Kids, 2018. 32p. (A Positive Power Story). $13.99. 9781623369538.
Multiple short sentences on each page, along with the repetition of words and illustrations that depict the text, make this level-two reader a good choice for kids looking for a little more challenge than a couple of words per page.

Scholastic Inc.—Scholastic Reader

Cox, Katherine. **The Lost Kitten.** Illustrated by Vanessa Brantley Newton. New York, NY: Scholastic Inc., 2015. 32p. (Katie Fry Private Eye). $3.99pa. 9780545666725pa.
A level-two reader that uses slightly longer sentences to increase the difficulty of the text.

Simon & Schuster—Ready to Read

DePaola, Tomie. **Strega Nona and Her Tomatoes.** New York, NY: Simon Spotlight, 2017. unpaged. (Strega Nona). $16.99. 9781481481359.
Strega Nona is a classic character that many parents and grandparents will remember from the picture book *Strega Nona*. Here, her personality shines through but the text has been modified so beginning readers will not be frustrated. A perk of this line is that it includes beloved characters like Ian Falconer's Olivia the pig and Cynthia Rylant's Henry and Mudge.

Non-Leveled Series

These books do not place a level on the cover but the beginning readers still focus on the elements that make books successful for kids learning to read. They cover a variety of stages, so becoming familiar with them will help you be better prepared to make suggestions to families.

Arnold, Tedd. **Fly Guy's Big Family.** New York, NY: Cartwheel Books, 2017. 30p. (Fly Guy). $6.99. 9780545663168.
The use of short chapters to tell the antics of Buzz and Fly Guy gives beginning readers the opportunity to read like a big kid. A good choice for both parents and kids who want chapter books before the child in question is really ready.

Butler, Dori Hillestad. **King & Kayla and the Case of the Missing Dog Treats.** Illustrated by Nancy Meyers. Atlanta, GA: Peachtree, 2017. 47p. (King & Kayla). $14.95. 9781561458776.
Just-enough clues are dropped to make the story interesting and keep the reader turning the page to see who the culprit is.

Jules, Jacqueline. **Sofia Martinez: Abuela's Special Letters.** Illustrated by Kim Smith. North Mankato, MN: Picture Window Books, 2017. 27p. (Sofia Martinez). $21.32. 9781515807285.

Introducing Spanish words into the story makes this series more accessible to English language learners. With many sentences per page, this series is for more advanced beginning readers.

Lin, Grace. **Ling & Ting: Not Exactly the Same!** New York, NY: Little, Brown and Company, 2010. 43p. (Ling & Ting). $14.99. 9780316024525.

There is still a lot of white space on the page but there are also more sentences, and the book is broken up into six chapters. This is just right for kids who are almost ready for a longer chapter book.

Pham, LeUyen. **The Itchy Book!** New York, NY: Hyperion Books for Children, 2018. 50p. (An Elephant & Piggie Like Reading! Book). $9.99. 9781368005647.

Playful, high-interest stories with colorful illustrations. Each book in the series is unrelated, and they are written by different authors. Pages with Mo Willems's Elephant and Piggie start and end each book.

Snyder, Laurel. **Charlie & Mouse.** Illustrated by Emily Hughes. San Francisco, CA: Chronicle Books, 2017. 37p. (Charlie and Mouse). $14.99. 9781452131535.

These two delightful brothers will steal the hearts of caregivers. There is a nostalgic feel to these books that portray everyday life for kids who do not have a lot of material things but do have great imaginations. The large amounts of white space on each page and between lines and individual words are just right for eyes trying to track words.

Thomas, Jan. **My Toothbrush Is Missing!** New York, NY: Houghton Mifflin Harcourt, 2018. unpaged. (Giggle Gang). $9.99. 9780544966352.

The comic style layout uses word bubbles to show which animal is speaking and the primary colors offset against a white word bubble and black text make this easy for those learning to read. At the end of the book, the author offers tips for how caregivers can successfully help their child learn to read.

Virján, Emma J. **What This Story Needs Is a Vroom and a Zoom.** New York, NY: Harper, 2017. unpaged. (Pig in a Wig). $9.99. 9780062494313.

The Pig in a Wig series is designed for kids just learning to pick out words on the page. There is a rhythm to the text that includes some rhyming words and repetitions of phrases. These components will help make the journey of learning to read successful.

Ziefert, Harriet. **Crab Cab.** Illustrated by Yukiko Kido. Maplewood, NJ: Blue Apple Books, 2014 (2008). unpaged. (Flip-a Word). $12.99. 9781609054304.

Few books do a better job of teaching kids word families. This series is a must for all libraries as they are the perfect books for parents who are ready to dive into teaching their child to read.

Chapter Books

Chapter books, even those for newly independent readers, should be housed in a different section than the beginning readers. These shorter chapter books can also be shelved separately from the longer, middle grade fiction. However, I would only recommend this if you have a sizable collection.

Chapter Books—Imprints

Some publishers will create imprints that focus on the chapter book reader. These chapter books are short, usually 100 pages or less, and they include illustrations, larger font, and more space between lines of text. Here are just a couple of standouts.

Branches—Scholastic. There are many series that fall under the umbrella of the Branches imprint. Branches books are created specifically for beginning chapter book readers, and the variety of genres increases the chances of kids finding titles they will enjoy reading. Although meant to be read by kids, they are also great to be read together until a kid becomes a more confident reader.

Lysiak, Hilde, and Matthew Lysiak. **Hero Dog!** Illustrated by Joanne Lew-Vriethoff. New York, NY: Branches, 2017. 102p. (Hilde Cracks the Case). $4.99pa. 9781338141559pa.
Hilde Lysiak is a kid author writing with her reporter father. Their series, Hilde Cracks the Case, falls into the mystery genre, and the character Hilde is a kid reporter and clue solver.

Aladdin QUIX—Simon & Schuster. The Aladdin QUIX line published their first three series in the fall of 2018. They are labeled as "Fast, Fun, Reads" and are just right for kids who need a short chapter book.

Quackenbush, Robert. **Express Train to Trouble.** New York, NY: Aladdin Quix, 2018 (1981). 64p. (A Miss Mallard Mystery). $16.99. 9781534414037.
George Ruddy Duck, a trickster who has been bothering all the train passengers, disappears, and mystery solver, Miss Mallard, must unravel the clues to discover what happened to him.

Chapter Books—First in Series

When kids move into chapter books, they typically become obsessed with series reading. They will find books they like and read everything in a series or by an author over and over again. Chapter books usually target the first-through third-grade age group. Some will be shorter at under 100 pages, and others will be more advanced and reach well over the 100-page mark.

Barkley, Callie. **Amy and the Missing Puppy.** Illustrated by Marsha Riti. New York, NY: Little Simon, 2013. 117p. (The Critter Club). $4.99pa. 9781442457690pa.

Girls volunteer at an animal shelter. The heavily illustrated pages, along with the subject matter, will draw in animal-loving readers.

Blabey, Aaron. **The Bad Guys.** New York, NY: Scholastic Inc., 2017 (2015). 139p. (The Bad Guys). $5.99pa. 9780545912402pa.

The Big Bad Wolf is trying to turn things around and has enlisted some of his fellow bad guys to help him change his behaviors. The humor is just right for a second or third grader, and with lots of illustrations and minimal text, this is a great starter chapter book series.

Citro, Asia. **Dragons and Marshmallows.** Illustrated by Marion Lindsay. Wood-inville, WA: The Innovation Press, 2017. 96p. (Zoey and Sassafras). $16.99. 9781943147083.

Zoey and her mother are the only ones who can see magical creatures, and it is their job to take care of them when they are hurt. A fantasy that is perfect for kids who have grown up watching Doc McStuffins and are ready for more content per page and less space between lines of text.

DiCamillo, Kate. **Mercy Watson to the Rescue.** Illustrated by Chris Van Dusen. Cambridge, MA: Candlewick Press, 2005. 69p. (Mercy Watson). $12.99. 9780763622701.

Feel-good stories about the beloved pig Mercy Watson who loves to eat hot toast with butter. The amusing antics are just right for kids looking for a funny chapter book.

Faruqi, Saadia. **Meet Yasmin!** Illustrated by Hatem Aly. North Mankato, MN: Picture Window Books, 2019. 89p. (Yasmini). $5.95pa. 9781684360222pa.

Yasmin is Pakistani American and she uses her creative mind to solve problems. This second grader is just the friend early chapter book readers are looking for. The colorful illustrations work well with the text and provide just enough clues to help new readers with words they might be unfamiliar with.

Gonzalez, Sarai, and Monica Brown. **Sarai and the Meaning of Awesome.** New York, NY: Scholastic Inc., 2018. 106p. (Sarai). $5.99pa. 978133823 6682pa.

Sarai is the child of immigrants and loves her close-knit family. When the house her grandparents have been renting is about to be sold out from under them, Sarai comes up with creative ways to buy it. The illustrations help bring life to the story.

Hale, Shannon, and Dean Hale. **The Princess in Black.** Illustrated by LeUyen Pham. Somerville, MA: Candlewick Press, 2014. 90p. (The Princess in Black). $14.99. 9780763665104.

A break from the stereotypical superhero story as this princess is the one in disguise and saving the day. Pull this one out when you have a child wanting a princess story and the parent does not or vice versa as it might just be the compromise that makes both parties happy.

James, Laura. **The Dog Who Sailed the Seas.** Illustrated by Eglantine Ceulemans. New York, NY: Bloomsbury Children's Books, 2017 (2016). 124p. (Captain Pug). $16.99. 9781681193809.
  A pampered pug gets separated from his girl and goes on an adventure to find her. A good fit for more sophisticated readers.
Klise, Kate. **Dying to Meet You.** Illustrated by M. Sarah Klise. Orlando, FL: Harcourt, 2009. 155p. (43 Cemetery Road). $15.00. 9780152057275.
  A series of epistolary novels with illustrations that tell the tale of a recluse writer named Ignatious B. Grumply, an abandoned 11-year-old named Seymour, and a ghost named Olive and how they become a family. Novels this length and style are best for kids just about ready to make the jump to middle grade fiction.
Krulik, Nancy. **Crash!** Illustrated by Louis Thomas. New York, NY: Grosset & Dunlap, 2017. 89p. (The Kid from Planet Z). $15.99. 9780448490137.
  Lots of white space and an illustration on each page make this science fiction series just right for kids ready to read a chapter book about aliens all by themselves.
LaReau, Kara. **The Infamous Ratsos.** Illustrated by Matt Myers. Somerville, MA: Candlewick Press, 2016. 58p. (The Infamous Ratsos). $14.99. 9780763676360.
  Short chapters with good spacing between lines give young eyes room to rest as they read about two brothers learning just what being brave and tough really means.
Pennypacker, Sara. **Waylon!: One Awesome Thing.** Illustrated by Marla Frazee. New York, NY: Disney Hyperion, 2016. 198p. (Waylon). $15.99. 9781484701522.
  Kids who gravitate toward science will appreciate the character of Waylon. At almost 200 pages, this book is the kind of story to give to kids looking for a book with a little more substance. There is a lot more text and fewer illustrations per page.
Springstubb, Tricia. **Cody and the Fountain of Happiness.** Illustrated by Eliza Wheeler. Somerville, MA: Candlewick Press, 2015. 151p. $14.99. 9780763658571.
  Realistic fiction tends to be a preference of many kids and caregivers. There is something comforting about reading about kids who act and have adventures similar to the reader's. Cody is this kind of character and her interest in ants and getting her older brother's attention will resonate with families. Makes a good read aloud, read together, or read independently depending on where the individual reader is at.
Urban, Linda. **Weekends with Max and His Dad.** Illustrated by Katie Kath. Boston, MA: Houghton Mifflin Harcourt, 2016. 150p. $16.99. 9780544598171.
  Three weekends worth of short stories detail Max's adventures with his newly divorced dad. The amount of text is greater than the number of illustrations. Give to kids dealing with their parents' divorce as well as those who like reading about neighborhood adventures.

Nonfiction

For some kids, learning to read may not start with fiction titles, especially for kids who are interested in animals and nature or have inquisitive minds. The need for engaging nonfiction books may be essential for helping these parents get their kids interested in the reading process.

I highly recommend that you pull out the beginning reader nonfiction titles. Branches at Cuyahoga County Public Library who have done this have seen an increase in the use of their nonfiction readers. Parents of nonfiction readers are happy not to have to hunt through more advanced books to find one of interest for their elementary-school reader. Beginning reader titles are identified by spines that have an F sticker along with a label that includes the call number and publication date.

Easy nonfiction is also appealing to emergent readers. These picture books use layouts and shorter texts that make them accessible to kids who are becoming more confident readers. Like a chapter book, easy nonfiction titles are for a more advanced reader and are books that can be read as a family or alone depending on the reader's ability.

Nonfiction Readers

As like fiction readers, these books may be leveled or not, but they all control the vocabulary of the books to make them accessible to those learning to read.

Bellwether Media—Blastoff Readers
Leaf, Christina. **Gray Squirrels.** Minneapolis, MN: Bellwether Media, 2015. 24p. (North American Animals). $25.95. 9781626171879.
> As a level three, the text is more involved and the sentences are more complex. The page layouts include box inserts that add to the text but do not busy the page.

HarperCollins—I Can Read
Driscoll, Laura. **I Want to Be a Doctor.** Illustrated by Catalina Echeverri. New York, NY: Harper, 2018. 31p. (My Community). $16.99. 9780062432414.
> This is a narrative nonfiction title. Since it reads more like fiction, it is likely to appeal to kids who like a good story and may not typically be drawn to nonfiction books.

Jump!—Bullfrog Books
Black, Vanessa. **Horses.** Minneapolis, MN: Bullfrog Books, 2017. 24p. (My First Pet). $25.65. 9781620315507.
> It starts with tips for parents, includes a table of contents, an index, and a glossary. The text includes short simple sentences, and photographs provide clues to unfamiliar words.

Kingfisher—Kingfisher Readers
Feldman, Thea. **Time.** New York, NY: Kingfisher, London, 2014. 32p. $12.99. 9780753471425.
> A beginning reader book with more than just a couple of words per page. For success, caregivers will want to read the note at the front. A nice feature is the bold vocabulary that is defined in the glossary in the back.

Lerner—Bumba Books
Flynn, Brendan. **Basketball Time!** Minneapolis, MN: Lerner Publications, 2017. 24p. $26.65. 9781512414325.
> Questions are posed throughout the text to engage adult and child when they read together. Short sentences and photographs make this an appealing choice for kids.

Lerner—First Step Nonfiction
Lindeen, Mary. **I Pick Fall Pumpkins.** Minneapolis, MN: Lerner Publications, 2017. 24p. $23.99. 9781512407969.
> A lot is packed into this little book. There is a table of contents, bolded vocabulary, vibrant photographs, and lots of white space around simple sentences.

Macmillan—My Readers
Macaulay, David, and Sheila Keenan. **Toilet: How It Works.** New York, NY: David Macaulay Studio, 2013. 32p. $15.99. 9781596437791.
> While still an early reader, this title is for kids who are reading pretty fluently on their own. There are short paragraphs that include complex sentences and more advanced vocabulary on each page.

National Geographic Kids—National Geographic Readers
Shields, Amy. **Trains.** Washington, DC: National Geographic Society, 2011. 32p. $3.99pa. 9781426307775pa.
> It is good to note the definition of the levels for these readers. The book states, "Level 1 books are just right for kids who are beginning to read on their own." I totally agree with this assessment and would just keep it in mind when thinking about the right reader to give it to.

Random House—Step into Reading
Ring, Susan. **Polar Bear Babies.** Illustrated by Lisa McCue. New York, NY: Random House, 2000. 32p. $12.99. 9780399549557.
> This level one reader's text offers lots of repetition to help build the confidence of the newest of readers and the white space and simple sentence make the layout just right.

Rodale Kids—Curious Readers

Carbone, Courtney. **This Makes Me Silly.** Illustrated by Hilli Kushnir. New York, NY: Rodale Kids, 2018. 32p. (Dealing with Feelings). $13.99. 9781635650754.

> A level two that has short sentences, usually two per page. The font size is a little smaller and the lines are closer together on the page. It makes it a just right read for kids looking for a more challenging beginning reader. This publisher is relatively new but the nonfiction readers are pretty impressive so far.

Treasure Bay Inc.—We Both Read

McKay, Sindy. **Habitats of the World.** Novato, CA: Treasure Bay, 2017. 41p. $9.95. 9781601152930.

> I love that these books promote reading together. Even a level-one book can pack in lots of facts but still be accessible to a novice reader.

Easy Nonfiction

Make sure you also consider your picture book nonfiction when reading and recommending. Look for books that have minimal text and lots of either photographs or illustrations. Kids can examine the images as they work to learn the words.

Alexander, Kwame. **Animal Ark: Celebrating Our Wild World in Poetry and Pictures.** Illustrated by Joel Sartore. Washington DC: National Geographic, 2017. unpaged. $15.99. 9781426327674.

> Haiku poems and close-up photographs introduce kids, in an accessible way, to animals from all over the world.

McCardie, Amanda. **Our Very Own Dog.** Illustrated by Salvatore Rubbino. Somerville, MA: Candlewick Press, 2016. 27p. $15.99. 9780763689483.

> This book demonstrates one child's experience with a new dog in text that beginning readers ready for sentences can handle. Also included, in a different font that is smaller in size, are tips parents can read about how to take care of a new pet dog.

Sayre, April Pulley, and Jeff Sayre. **Warbler Wave.** New York, NY: Beach Lane Books, 2018. unpaged. $17.99. 9781481448291.

> Sparse text shares the life of the warbler bird. Some of the words may require a little help from a grown-up, but it will increase a child's vocabulary.

Programs and Services for the Beginning Reader

For caregivers of beginning readers, navigating the library's shelves and collections can be difficult. One option might be to create a system that lumps the reader section by the stage a reader is at. For caregivers with kids who are excelling at learning to read, they may need librarian intervention to keep the book selections age appropriate. Librarians can help caregivers consider the appropriateness of theme and layout, not just reading level.

Color-Coded Readers—Multnomah County Library, Oregon

Libraries are always looking for ways to help kids and parents find the right books to take home. Making it easier to find books for kids learning to read can make the library experience more enjoyable for families. To do this, some libraries are creating their own systems to help caregivers identify books on a certain topic or, in this case, their proficiency in reading.

Background

Multnomah County Library has spent the last 15 years focusing on early childhood but the focus ended at kindergarten. Recently, they decided to broaden the focus and a team of staff got together to imagine ways to bridge the years from kindergarten to third grade, the time period that many kids go from the learning to read stage to the reading to learn stage of childhood.

Their number-one goal was to leverage the resources of the public library to parents and schools in order to support the learning-to-read process. They were finding that the books kids were using to learn to read at school were focused on specific skills rather than characters, plots, and illustration. Since Multnomah had already invested heavily in beginning readers as well as beginning facts (nonfiction beginning readers), it was logical to try to make more educators and families aware of these collections.

The Nuts and Bolts

Over a five-year process and with a grant from the Paul Allen Family Foundation that lasted for the first three years, the library set out to work with the eight school districts they serve. They were looking to find where the gaps were in the learning-to-read continuum and then exploring ways to fill them. The ultimate goal was to leverage the resources of the public library to support students and families in their learning-to-read journey.

To get the venture underway, the library's project team created a survey that they shared with 400 kindergartens through third-grade teachers, reading specialists, and administrators. Following the survey, the library used qualitative interviews with individual educators to test the quantitative results. Now they had real data to help them see where they needed to put their time, energy, and financial resources.

Some key findings from the educational research study:

- Almost half of the teachers (46%) say more of their students are struggling with reading today.
- Ninety-three percent of teachers say they strongly agree that they wish every reluctant reader in their classroom could get personal help choosing books that will spark their interest in reading.
- Eighty-five percent say the library plays a crucial role in helping parents engage in their children's development as readers (O'Dell 2018).

It became clear that one of their goals needed to be making the beginning reader section of the library more prominent and user friendly. Now they just had to figure out the best way to do it.

Color Coding the Beginning Reader Collection

During those first few years, Multnomah County Library was able to use some of the grant funding to add a reading specialist to the library's staff. Having a specialist in the area of how to teach reading was a huge asset for the library. He was able to help them better understand what it entails to learn to read and come up with ways to express this to parents and even teachers.

The first thing the reading specialist did was an ethnographic study of each of Multnomah County Library's 19 locations' beginning reader collections. He spent 90 minutes in each space observing how the collection was being used by kids, parents and kids, and parents, kids, and librarians. What he discovered was that within 15 seconds or less, kids would accept or return a book based on what was inside. They would keep looking until they found the book that had the right balance of words, white space, and illustration that felt like a good fit.

He also noticed that this did not really change when the librarian was present because while they are readers themselves, it is hard to be an expert on all the different levels and layouts found in a beginning reader. Unless the new reader had a specific character or series in mind, staff were still doing a hunt-and-peck style just like the kids and parents. With this knowledge in hand, the task then became how to ease this situation without pigeonholing a kid's book choices.

Process for Color Coding

The programming and outreach director for Multnomah County Library, Katie O'Dell, saw things start to come together when the project team began to think about what kids needed on the page at the different stages of learning to read. It was all about page layout, the number of words per page, the size of illustration, and not so much about what the level on the book might be.

In the end, Multnomah settled on four color-coded categories for their beginning readers. A DIY board with the four categories was created and then the project team had staff practice with a stack of books. They were satisfied that they were on the right track when both groups were putting the majority of the books in the same categories.

Implementing the Color-Code System

Once the color categories were decided upon, it was time to overhaul the entire fiction beginning reader collection at all 19 branches. Colored tape was purchased to apply to the spines of the book. The books are shelved by the color tape and then the author. This would make the browsing quicker and more successful. Nonfiction books were not included in the color coding because the team knew from research that new readers stretch themselves more to read a fact book that is of high interest, even if it is a challenge for them.

Books Already in the Collection. To start, a big weed was done at the branches to remove books that were not circulating or were in poor condition. You do not want to spend the staff time it would take to relabel these books. From there a team of six people made up of branch, cataloging, collection development, and processing staff started at the largest branch. They touched each book and evaluated it. A decision was made, a label was placed on the spine, and the catalog was changed. They moved to each branch, and after that, they were able to scan barcodes to see if a title had already been re-cataloged. If it had, they just needed to add the color label and move on. More and more titles would just need the color label as the project advanced.

New Titles Being Added to the Collection. After the initial relabeling project was complete, the decision for new books is made when the book arrives, not when it is ordered. The processing department, they do their own processing of materials, uses the DIY board to help them determine a book's color. If needed, they ask the youth materials selector for input. For the most part, they have found that the processing staff can go by the previous series designation because all the beginning readers in a series would be in the same category.

Taking It a Step Further

After the collection was relabeled toward the end of 2017, the staff team at Multnomah decided to create kits with five titles that fall into a specific color category. Along with the books, a list of reading tips and suggestions for more titles the reader might like are included. A survey for parents to fill out is also part of the kit. Currently, Multnomah has about 2,000 kits spread across 19 branches. The biggest challenge is that the kits, which are in bags, take up a lot of space and are hard to house on regular shelving.

Making room for these kits has paid off as the survey results from parents have shown that:

- Ninety-two percent found it easy to find the right kit for their child.
- Eight out of ten said their children enjoyed most of the books.
- Parents noted an unexpected benefit: opening the kit filled with books provides an element of surprise and discovery that gets children excited about reading, even before they dive into the books (O'Dell 2018).

Promotional Materials

Bookmarks were created that customers can take with them that explain the new color-coded system. Signs at the beginning reader section, as shown in Figure 3.1, also carry this information.

Figure 3.1   Color-Coded Readers Sign

Reprinted with permission from Multnomah County Library.

Making It Work for Your Library

The scale of creating a color-coded system at your library, whether it is a school or public library, will depend on the size of your library system and the size of your collection. One of the first things I would recommend doing is meeting with your administrators to discuss the potential benefits and find out what concerns there might be. It is always a good idea to have this conversation up front so there are fewer surprises later on. Once you have the green light, it is time to consider putting together your team of people to help with the process as well as spreading the word to parents and teachers.

Public Libraries. It will likely mean working with your cataloging and processing departments during the rebranding process and when future picks are added. If your library has the cataloging and processing of materials done by a vendor, that will be an added challenge. Most likely, you will still need to add the color tape or label of your choice when the books arrive, and if you want it reflected in the catalog, you will need to have access to updating your own records.

If your collections float between branches, this is an additional piece to consider. You will need to have a process for catching items that float to branches that have already been rebranded so they can be fixed. If your collections do not float, but you have multiple branches, then you will have to decide if all books will have the same label or if individual branches can make their own decisions. My recommendation is that you try to standardize, especially if it will be included in the online catalog. This will help caregivers feel more confident in trusting your system.

Another consideration for libraries that do centralized selection will be how to determine what color label a book gets. At Cuyahoga County Public Library, I determine what labels a book gets and I do it at the point of ordering. We have 28 locations and the cataloging of a book is the same for each location. To have the cataloging or processing departments take on the role of decision maker would be a change in job duties. If your library is in this situation, you definitely want to have the conversation with administrators early on so this piece can be mapped out to the agreement of all involved.

School Libraries. If you are in a large school district, you may or may not find it necessary to have all the school libraries use the same system and catalog each book in the same way. If you choose to go with a standard system, and you have more than one school librarian, this is likely to take lots of discussion to determine best practices. Writing down what is agreed upon is an excellent way to cut down on misremembering later on. If you are a single elementary school or the only librarian for a district, you will still want to create the categories you are planning to use so teachers, kids, and caregivers will be able to understand your system and thought process.

The big challenge for a school library is probably finding the time to do a large overhaul of the collection in between library instruction and class visits to check out materials. You will want to work out this piece with your administration, especially if you might need to limit access to parts of the library for short periods of time or if you want to work on the project when school is not in session, like spring break or summer vacation.

Decision Time

If a complete overhaul is more than you want to take on right now, you might still consider creating some kits based on the four categories that Multnomah County Library created. This is a way to support the needs of the people you serve and can be created with books already in your school or public library collection. You will need to invest in bags or boxes to house the items in. Just remember they take up space and may not fit on your regular shelving so plan accordingly.

Ultimately, you will need to decide if adding a more structured system that considers where the child is at on his or her journey to being a reader is right for your library. Whatever you decide, I recommend you not use the word level in your system. The word is loaded and can cause negative responses from the community.

ABC Book Club—Cuyahoga County Public Library, Ohio, Olmsted Falls Branch

Many libraries offer book discussions for school age kids. Typically, a school age book discussion will start around third grade, then there might be ones for teens, and of course for adults. However, few libraries think to have book discussions with beginning readers like those in kindergarten. The Olmsted Falls Branch entered into a partnership with the Early Childhood Center to create such a program.

Background

The library was actually approached by the director of the Early Childhood Center, Melinda Falconi, who runs the preschool through kindergarten program for the Olmsted Falls City Schools. She had noticed that there were no reading programs for kids in kindergarten who were already reading. The initial idea for the book discussion club was to start a program for these specific kids.

Falconi found that parents of kindergarten readers were already stopping reading aloud to their children simply because they could read on their own. These parents were also moving their five-year-old children to chapter books rather than beginning readers or even picture books. So the base-level goal of the program was to keep families reading together as kids developed as individual readers.

Program Basics

The book discussion for kindergarteners and caregivers was first offered in 2014. Sue Grame is the children's librarian currently working with Falconi, but the program originated with the previous children's librarian Michelle Todd. Forming the program created a strong partnership between the library and the local schools. Each ABC Book Club is planned and attended by the public library's children's librarian and the director of the Olmsted Falls Early Childhood Center, and they run from October through May.

At the start of each school year, Grame shares possible titles in a meeting with Falconi. They settle on titles and then share their ideas over e-mail or before and after an evening's book discussion. Grame tries to pick newer titles, but they have done some older titles and have even repeated ones that worked really well in previous years. They use both fiction and nonfiction picture books and discuss the different ways you can approach each type of book. Like with nonfiction, you can sometimes dip in and out of the book rather than having to read it from front to back straight through.

They each plan and present parts of the ABC Book Club. Creating engaging questions for the families around the book is done by Falconi. Things that tend to be covered when discussing the book are vocabulary, setting, characters, title, author, illustrator, and even the dedication. It is important to look at it as a whole unit and talk about all the parts that make up a book. Craft planning and finding a tie to the Common Core Standards comes from Grame. A hands-on activity helps make the book stick in a child's mind longer. She also works with the collection development department to acquire enough copies of each title.

The first book is given out at the first meeting of the year. This means that families have not had a chance to read it yet. As a group, they read the book a couple of times to help with comprehension. The first reading tends to be with no pictures so the focus is on the words and families imagining what is happening. The second reading is with pictures and they learn if the meaning of the story changes based on the images provided by the illustrator.

After that, books are given out at the end of each month's discussion. Families are asked to commit to coming each month and to reading and re-reading the month's selection prior to attending the ABC Book Club so that kids have a chance to become familiar with both the words and the pictures.

Promotion

Originally, teachers were asked to identify kids and a note was sent home to invite them to participate in the ABC Book Club. Over time, they opened the program up to all library users in the age group through the library's online event calendar. While the focus in the beginning was for advanced readers, that has shifted and kids at various stages of learning to read are now welcomed. They still keep it strictly to kids in kindergarten.

To help get the word out, Cuyahoga County Public Library's graphics department created bookmarks. The bookmarks list all the meeting dates for the year along with the titles and covers for each book that will be discussed. Having the bookmark is a personal touch that parents appreciate, and they can stick it on the refrigerator or clip it to the family calendar.

Parent Participation

The ABC Book Club is a book discussion for both the child and the parent. Both the grown-up and the kindergartener are asked to answer book-related questions and to make the craft. Just like in storytime, they want the parents to recognize the importance of continuing to read with their new readers, to make sure they see that challenging their beginning readers is okay but that leaping into chapter books needs to be done in an age-appropriate way. While a truly gifted reader might be able to tackle the text in J. K. Rowling's *Harry Potter and the Sorcerer's Stone* at five, the context and comprehension of that text is potentially beyond a five-year-old's grasp.

Parents who are watchers or listeners at first will, over time, start to open up and engage with the kids and the program presenters. Grame has also observed that the way Falconi talks to the kids is very important. She does not talk down to them but instead uses long words and offers lots of context to develop a kid's vocabulary.

Since the program has a limit of 12 kids and their parents, the group has a chance to bond with each other. As they meet month after month, they become familiar with the process of the program and interacting with books with their child. Grame also notes that kids connect with her outside of the program. They talk to her when they visit the library and when she comes to visit their school.

Incorporating at Your Library

This is one program that is easy to adopt at just about any public or school library. Whether you are able to partner with your counterpoint or not, you can reach kindergarten-age families. The budget is pretty minimal and most of the cost is optional. The only must is the cost of supplies for the craft or an activity. The expenses can be kept low by the decisions you make on what type of materials you will use. Some of the other optional expenses include providing a snack like cookies and small bottles of water. Grame sets aside $75 for a special final program like bringing in a local author or having the kids create their own ABC book that is bound for the end-of-year celebration.

Public Library. The Friends of the Library can usually help cover the cost of craft materials and snacks. If money for a last hurrah program in May cannot be acquired, it is not necessary for the program to take place. If relationships with the local school system prevent a partnership for presenting, the children's staff can do all of the planning and presenting. However, having that school and public library connection is wonderful so think outside the box and try to make it happen when you can.

School Library. Budgets for extra supplies and snacks can be more challenging for school librarians. A possible avenue might be the Parent Teacher Association or the equivalent in your school district. If not, keep the crafts super simple or partner with the art teacher. You can also skip the snacks and special celebration and just focus on the joy of reading.

If time allows you might partner with the kindergarten teachers to present and have the caregivers invited to the school once a month for book club or it could be an afterschool or evening program. Coming from the public library side, I would also suggest reaching out to your public library counterpart. Many children's librarians would be thrilled to come to the schools to help present, provide the multiple copies of books needed, and help share costs.

Building Your Readers Advisory Toolbox

Reading up on various leveling systems will better prepare you when families come in looking for a beginning reader with only a few words per page versus a beginning reader book that has multiple sentences per page or vice versa.

- Read one nonleveled beginning reader per quarter.
- Read one early chapter book per quarter.
- Read a dozen fiction and nonfiction leveled beginning readers each year. Mix it up between publishers and levels each month.
- Read a couple of Holiday House's "I Like to Read" books that use the Fountas and Pinnell leveling system in a year.

References

Article

Parrott, Kiera. "Fountas and Pinnell Lament Labels." *School Library Journal* 63, no. 11 (November 2017): 15.

Book

Rowling, J. K. **Harry Potter and the Sorcerer's Stone**. Illustrated by Mary GrandPré. New York, NY: Arthur A. Levine Books, 1998 (1997). 309p. (Harry Potter). $26.99. 9780590353403.

Interviews

Gillis, Jessica. In e-mail interview with the author. September 21, 2018.
Grame, Sue. In interview with the author. May 8, 2018.
O'Dell, Katie. In phone interview with the author. April 30, 2018.

Website

"Welcome to the (Theodor Seuss) Geisel Award home page!" *Association for Library Service to Children*. Accessed September 6, 2018. http://www.ala .org/alsc/awardsgrants/bookmedia/geiselaward.

Additional Readings

Articles

Clark, Summer. "What My First Grader Taught Me About Reading." *Horn Book Magazine* 93, no. 5 (September 2017): 42–46.
Parrott, Kiera. "Thinking Outside the Bin." *School Library Journal* 63, no. 8 (August 2017): 42–45.
Scheuer, Mary Ann. "Beyond Reading Levels: Choosing Nonfiction for Developing Readers." *School Library Journal, News & Features*. August 28, 2017. https://www.slj.com/?detailStory=beyond-reading-levels-choosing-non fiction-for-developing-readers.

CHAPTER FOUR

Supporting Parents of Developing Readers

This chapter was originally going to be titled "Supporting Parents When a Child Is a Struggling Reader," but that changed after hearing the author and national ambassador for Young People's Literature Jacqueline Woodson's reasons against using the "struggling reader" label. She talks about kids like her who are "reading slowly and deliberately and deconstructing language" and how this slowness is considered a problem by adults (Iasevoli 2018). Woodson makes the case that the ability to read changes over time and trying to put kids into neat little boxes can have a detrimental effect on a kid's sense of self.

This struck a chord with me because I've always considered myself a child who struggled to learn to read. I personally had two challenges to overcome. I have weak eye muscles, and it made it hard to focus on the page without getting lost among the words. Lucky for me, my mother noticed the problem and she took me to the eye doctor. Getting glasses made a big difference.

My second challenge was a bigger hurdle to get over. I was not, and to this day am not, phonetic. My mother, who taught preschool at the time, had the educational background to help me. She had learned that kids are ready to start learning to read at different times. She also knew that seeing and hearing words would build my vocabulary to the point that reading would click even if sounding out words never came easy. In her career as a preschool, kindergarten, and third-grade teacher, she witnessed this over and over again in her students. For me, it did click—sometime during the second grade. After that, I became a voracious reader, but the path to being a successful reader is different for every child.

When Reading Is Not Happening as Expected

If learning to read was not a challenge for you, it might be difficult to relate to someone who tussles with the written word. While this can be true for some librarians, it can be even more of an issue for caregivers. Frustration levels can run high, but the right tone at the library can make a huge difference. As someone who took a zigzagging path to reading, I consider these kids near and dear to my heart.

Roadblocks to Reading Success

When a child is not learning to read at the same speed as a friend, sibling, or classmate, it can be hard on both the parent and the child. Many times, there is absolutely nothing amiss, and other times there may be an underlying cause or disability. A couple of areas that kids can fall into include:

- Slow starter—These kids are just not meant to read before kindergarten or to be a fluent reader by the end of first grade. Given time and support, they will develop their reading skills and become proficient readers.
- Medical reason—This could be dyslexia, a visual impairment, or something else completely.

Librarians are not meant to diagnose the problem. Instead, librarians can offer encouragement and suggest things like checking with a child's teacher, pediatrician, or eye doctor for feedback. It is important to let the professionals work with families to identify any reasons why reading might be more challenging for an individual child. If needed, a plan can be put in place by these experts to help the child feel more positive about the reading process. Hopefully, one part of the plan will be visits to the local library for books and other resources. When that happens, you will need to be prepared to work with families who are under more stress than the average family.

Tips for Concerned Parents

Both the parent and the child in a developing reader situation can be feeling embarrassed when they arrive at the reference desk. A key thing to remember is that this a sensitive conversation. Caregivers can be on the defense even when you are only trying to get the basic facts about why they have come to visit, let alone when you might offer some advice. On a first visit, just stick with something as simple as "what do you like to do for fun." Then find a book on the topic that excites the child and that he or she can practice reading with. If you can, throw in one that is on the same topic but that a caregiver would need to read aloud or that comes as an audiobook (just make sure to include the print book too).

Reading Aloud

No matter the age of the child, reading aloud is super important. Woodson talks about this important activity in relation to teachers reading aloud to their students but it is just as crucial for the parent-and-child relationship. These are some phrases I like to use with caregivers as we develop a relationship and the situation presents itself.

- Reading aloud at any age is a great way to make books a pleasurable experience. Many adults like to listen to audiobooks during their commute or when they workout. Kids also like hearing a story, and that joy does not end when they age out of storytime or can read on their own.
- Read a chapter or two at a time and then discuss what happened. This will help build comprehension as a part of the reading experience.
- Over time, start having your child read a few words, a couple of sentences, a paragraph, or a page to help boost fluency and make the time together more of an interaction.

Working with Developing Reader Families

When a new family enters the library, it may be the only time you see them. They may be visiting from out of town or simply visiting from a neighboring community. It might be a Tuesday morning when you always work, but in the future, the family will only be able to come on Thursday evenings when you are not on the schedule. No matter what, you want to provide the best customer-centered experience you can so that the library as an institution becomes a place the family wants to return to.

Taking the time to listen and perhaps go the extra mile to get a child the book they really want can go a long way with parents. Bringing your own enthusiasm about books into the conversation can be contagious, and it models for caregivers how they can in turn talk about books with their kids at home. Your interactions may last only a few minutes or could go on for a half hour. Busy librarians may have to step away to help another family, but you always want to check back and make sure no one goes home discouraged.

Working with a Family

Recently when working the reference desk, I had a mother with three girls approach me. All of her girls were reading below grade level and the mother wanted help finding books for them. I suggested we all go over and look for books together in the easy-reader section. We took a peek inside a few books so I could gauge how many words/sentences on the page the kids were comfortable with. I wanted to error on the side of perhaps a little too easy in order to help build a little confidence. From there, I started doing readers advisory interviews with the girls one at a time in order to see what they were most interested in—princesses, animals, cars, and so on—and then matched each girl up with three books to take home.

Once the girls had their books, the mother asked for help choosing a book to read aloud as a family. At first, I suggested a chapter book but the mother resisted. Perhaps she was not a strong reader herself or the girls simply had short attention spans. I did not push it with the mother but instead took them over to the new picture book display. We found a couple of possibilities before the mother remembered the stripes book that the girls really liked. It took a little back-and-forth conversation to realize she meant David Shannon's *A Bad Case of Stripes*. I did not have a copy available that day, but it ended up being a win-win situation as a hold was placed and they checked out a few new titles to help tide them over.

The most rewarding part of the exchange came when the family went to check out the books. The oldest girl was super-protective of her picks. She made sure her books did not get mixed in with her sisters'. Both the mother and the girls left feeling jazzed about their reading choices rather than feeling bad about any reading challenges they had. That, of course, is always the goal when working with kids and their parents, but even more so when a child is feeling overwhelmed by the challenge of learning to read.

Working with an Individual Child and Parent

One afternoon I received a phone call from a children's assistant at one of the branch libraries I select books for. She was an experienced recommender of books, but she was in a quandary with her latest mother and daughter customers. The daughter was dyslexic and reading was hard for her. The layout of a beginning reader was best for her, but as a middle grader, she wanted to be reading what her friends were reading.

After doing some research, the staff member had found a series CreateSpace had just started publishing called DyslexiAssist. CreateSpace self-publishes books and the quality of the books published can vary greatly. It is not a publisher I tend to gravitate toward when I'm purchasing materials for Cuyahoga County Public Library, except in specific circumstances. This proved to be one of those exceptions.

There were only a few books in the series at the time but I ordered several copies of each. All branch staff were alerted to the purchase in case they had similar customers who could benefit. These books look similar to what a middle grade reader would be reading but have more white space on the page and more space between the lines so they are easier for a dyslexic reader. The mother and the daughter were both delighted when the books arrived in the branch a couple of weeks later. DyslexiAssist met an immediate need, but I began looking for other options and found some in large print and e-books.

Collection Development and Merchandising: Alternate Formats

The alternate formats that a library carries can make a great impact on the reading skills and habits of a child that will stay with them clear into adulthood. When caregivers share information about their child's reading troubles or the challenges he or she faces, it is an opportunity for librarians to step in and suggest a format that might be more conducive to an individual child's learning style.

Large Print Collections

Developing readers are not stupid but they may feel that way because of the specific challenges they have to overcome in order to make reading enjoyable instead of a chore to get through. Having a children's large print collection can serve several purposes to help improve the reading experience for the parent and child.

1. It allows visually impaired kids to be able to read the books their friends are reading.
2. It makes it possible for adults who want to read along with the kids in their life but need a larger font to do so.
3. It uses a layout that helps kids who process the written word differently.

At my library, we had purchased large print regularly in the 1990s and early 2000s. They were mostly classic titles, but the collection had not been updated much until 2017. We had picked up adult crossover titles like *Fault in Our Stars* by John Green, and these copies did circulate well for us. This mix of older classic titles and the few new titles seemed to meet the demand.

Then I attended a Baker and Taylor and Thorndike Press webinar "Engaging Reluctant Readers in Your Library" and began to realize our developing readers could have the opportunity to read the same books as their peers, if they were in a larger font, had more space between lines, and had more white space on the page (Grice, Joyce, and McAlpine 2018). After all, this is what the best beginning reader books offer children. I decided to test this out by adding new core titles to the collection.

The scope and nature of the titles I choose for the initial order, as seen in Appendix B, provided a nice collection for testing the waters and assessing the needs of the community. I selected titles by authors like Jeff Kinney, J. K. Rowling, and Rick Riordan. These authors write popular middle grade reads and would allow a developing reader the opportunity to grab books like the ones their friends are reading. It was a big first order, and after that, a handful of titles have been added each year.

I purchased four copies of each title and targeted four branches where the children tend to need support when it comes to reading. These books were labeled with our LP sticker and were given a large print location code in our ILS system, Innovative Interfaces Inc.'s Sierra. This helps for both online and library browsing. The other decision made was to shelve the large print books side by side with their typical hardback counterpart. My goal was to make these accessible to readers when they were browsing and to cut down on the otherness of the books.

The large print titles are circulating throughout all 28 branches thanks to floating. When reports were run in August 2018, 63 percent of the collection that was added in October 2017 was checked out. The Diary of a Wimpy Kid series had the highest turnover with titles circulating at anywhere from 9 to 15 time per copy. Additional circulation statistics can be found in Table 4.1.

Shortly after adding these large print titles to the collection, a teacher came in looking for large print titles for a visually impaired student at her school. She was thrilled to find that *Wonder* by R. J. Palacio was in large print. Her class was reading it, and now all the students would be able to

Table 4.1   Kid's Large Print Statistics

Kids Large Print Statistics
Cuyahoga County Public Library
October 2017–August 2018

42	Number of titles purchased	
167	Number of copies purchased	
16	Number of copies missing, billed, or damaged	10%
151	Number of copies still in circulation	90%
106	Number of copies checked out	63%
45	Number of copies check shelf	27%
6	Average number of circulations per copy October 2017–August 2018	

read it together. We showed her how to search the catalog for other large print titles for her student to enjoy. Staff are also making an effort to highlight the large print titles, with readers needing a little more help.

e-Book Collections

Your electronic collections are a treasure trove of materials with customization features a print book does not have. Adult librarians have seen their seniors using the e-reader font-enhancing feature for years so they can mimic large print books. I am still a print-book reader at heart, but the ability to enlarge text is a perfect feature to use with kids who need a little additional help to be effective readers.

No matter your personal opinion about e-books, you should take the time to learn the features of your e-book vendor's app for font type and size. Cuyahoga County uses Overdrive and its app does allow the customization of size and font for most books. They call it text scale and book design on their Libby app and they also offer a font called OpenDyslexic for anyone with dyslexia or who might benefit from its design. This font choice puts more space between words and lines of text and also weighs the bottom of each word with a heavier use of ink.

Audiobook Collections

While an adult reading aloud to a child is the preferred method for sharing a book out loud, it might not always be an option. When it's not, audiobooks are a nice substitute and can even help build a reader's confidence over time. As McGuire states, "Audiobooks can also be a way of introducing books above your child's current reading level, so that more complex stories and vocabulary can be introduced and enjoyed" (McGuire 2013). If a child is auditory, it will be even more helpful to listen to the words rather than just see the printed form. When families go in this direction, make sure you give them both the print book and the audiobook.

Read-along options are available for young children and usually include a picture book or beginning reader along with a CD or a playaway. They can also be an option with your e-content vendor. Once books move into the middle grade arena or higher, libraries usually do not buy the book and audiobook as a packaged set, and at Cuyahoga County Public Library, we do not interfile the audiobook copies with the books. We do it this way because the audiobooks can get lost on the shelves among the books and also because there are kids and adult listeners who want an audiobook and prefer to browse just that particular format.

When the two formats are not shelved together, librarians will need to help families take that extra step to match them up. Summer is also a great time to create a display of books and audiobooks together so families can grab and go. Here are some excellent choices that the family can enjoy together.

Excellent Narrator

The right narrator will make an audiobook hard to turn off.

Riordan, Rick. **The Lightning Thief.** Read by Jesse Bernstein. New York, NY: Listening Library, 2005. unabridged. (Percy Jackson and the Olympians). $40.00. 9780307245304.
Percy Jackson learns he is a demigod in this mix of modern day and Greek mythology.
Rowling, J. K. **Harry Potter and the Sorcerer's Stone.** Read by Jim Dale. New York, NY: Listening Library, 1999. unabridged. (Harry Potter). $60.00. 9780807286005.
Harry Potter's adventures begin when he gets his letter to the Hogwarts School of Witchcraft and Wizardry.

Sound Effects and Musical Accompaniments

Adding the right extras to an audiobook makes listening almost like a cinematic experience.

Colfer, Eoin, and Andrew Donkin. **Illegal.** Read by Ensemble Cast. Chicago, IL: Dreamscape Media, 2018. unabridged. $64.99. 9781974924592.
Ebo makes the treacherous journey from Ghana to Europe in search of his sister and brother.
Ryan, Pam Muñoz. **Echo.** Read by Mark Bramhall, David De Vries, MacLeod Andrews, and Rebecca Sole. New York, NY: Scholastic Audio, 2015. unabridged. $39.99. 9780545788366.
Multiple story lines that take place during different periods of history are woven together through a harmonica.

Engaging Stories

An action-packed narrative will keep listeners engaged.

Brown, Peter. **The Wild Robot.** Read by Kate Atwater. New York, NY: Hachette Audio, 2016. unabridged. (Wild Robot). $25.00. 9781478938354.
An orphaned gosling imprints on a robot, and they adapt to life together on a deserted island.

Reynolds, Jason. **Ghost.** Read by Guy Lockard. New York, NY: Simon & Schuster Inc., 2016. unabridged. (Track). $64.99. 9781508230489.
Ghost is fast on the track, but learning you cannot outrun your bad
choices is a lesson he still needs to learn.

Programs to Support Developing Readers

Libraries have an opportunity to support school age kids needing to
improve their reading skills in order to reach grade-level proficiency. Many
for-profit options are available to families, but libraries have the ability to
offer these programs at no charge. The level of reading coaching that a library
offers will vary, but no matter the size or type of library, there is an option
for you.

FOG Readers—San Francisco Public Library, California

The cost of a reading tutor for a child is very expensive, and not every
family can afford it. Parents are thrilled when their library can provide a
similar service for free, but to do so can be costly. If your library is looking to
offer a tutoring service to families with kids who need a little extra help, San
Francisco Public Library has laid the groundwork for you.

Background

In 2017, Laura Lay, the learning differences librarian at San Francisco
Public Library, started FOG Readers to help first to fourth graders improve
their reading skills. Lay had previously worked at a nonprofit where parents
could pay $60 to $100 an hour for a tutor to work one-on-one with their
child to improve literacy skills like phonics and fluency. However, many
families could not afford this expensive program for their children. When
Lay started with San Francisco Public Library in 2015, one of her goals was
to bring a free version of this program to library customers.

Why FOG Readers?

Besides wanting to equalize the access to a phonics-based program, there
were several other reasons that helped Lay make her case. The first is that
one in five children have been diagnosed with dyslexia and the materials to
be used in FOG had already been proven to help dyslexic readers. Second,
50 percent of the third and fourth graders in San Francisco were reading
below grade level. Lastly, whether a child was reading below grade level
because of a learning challenge like dyslexia, a poor foundation of literacy

skills, or because English was not the child's first language, a program like FOG could help them all.

The Program, Materials, and Budget

The foundation for the program used at San Francisco comes from the Institute for Multi-Sensory Education's Orton-Gillingham program. The training is offered all over the country, but it is a little expensive at $1,200 for 30 hours of training over the course of five days.

Lay already had this training when she started at the library. If your library does not have the financial resources to send someone to training, an alternative could be working with a reading teacher or specialist at your local schools. Through discussions you could create your own curriculum and lesson plans for tutors. San Francisco has also started sharing their curriculum with other libraries.

Participation—Parent/Child

As of March 2018, there have been 126 pairs matched up and 109 were active at 23 of San Francisco Public Library's 28 branches. The pairs meet together at a library branch for 45 minutes to 1 hour of one-on-one tutoring each week. Ongoing sessions allow for a relationship to develop and for the child to become more comfortable reading aloud to their tutor. For most children it takes about one year to get through the first two levels of the five-level program and go from learning to read to reading to learn. From here children may graduate from the program and tutors can be matched up with new students. If the tutor and the family want to continue to levels three through five, that is also an option.

Participation—Tutor

Tutors are asked to commit to at least six months when they sign up to volunteer. They are fingerprinted and FBI background checked. Initially tutors were found through Volunteer Match, and many still find out about the program this way, but as FOG has grown so has word-of-mouth advertisement from the current group of tutors. Interestingly, the majority of tutors are millennials from the tech industry who were not regular library users before volunteering. Instead, they have found the program because they are interested in giving back to their community. This ended up being a wonderful opportunity to sign up new library card users and introduce the volunteers to other aspects of the library.

In order to become a tutor, volunteers must attend four one-and-a-half-hour sessions that are offered once a month by Lay. Once completed, the tutors are matched with a child. During these sessions, the tutors learn the basics of the program and how to use the information with the child they are matched up with. Parents are invited to the tutor training so they can see the bones of the program their child will be going through.

Making It Happen

FOG Readers is a wonderful way to make an impact in the community and help kids develop as readers. However, you might not have the staffing or financial resources to implement at your library. Not to worry. There are other ways to reach families in need that are less staff- and financially intense.

One way would be to have homework mentors who are available after school to help any child with his or her homework. This can be done with volunteers or paid employees. Cuyahoga County offers homework mentors at 14 branches that do not have homework centers. Homework center branches have a homework coordinator for the site along with tutors who can help with assignments. These are paid positions, usually grant funded, but volunteers can also be used. The difference is that they help with homework rather than tutor to improve specific skills. Depending on the number of kids needing homework help on any given day, the homework mentors or homework center staff will work one-on-one or in small groups to help kids with school assignments. All volunteers and hired staff are background checked.

Book Buddies with Foster Grandparents—Warren-Trumbull County Public Library, Ohio, Main Library

During my time as a children's librarian, I ran a book buddies program in the summer. For six weeks, first through third graders could practice their reading with a big book buddy who was usually a middle- or high-school student. Book buddies can also be done with adults acting as the big buddies. Practicing reading with a nonparent can dial down the anxiety that can develop at home.

Background

The Family and Community Services Inc. program coordinator of Foster Grandparents contacted Lori about having their foster grandparent volunteers work with kids at the library. Lori immediately thought of her book buddies program as a natural fit. The foster grandparents typically work with kids in schools, so they would be great listeners for the kids practicing their reading.

Planning

The wonderful thing about a book buddies program is that it truly needs minimal preparation and funding, so it works for all types and sizes of libraries. You just need kids to read and someone to listen to them. Preferably one-on-one, but I have had situations where we had to double up the little buddies or the big buddies depending on who showed up that day.

Staff will need to pull a variety of books from the collection for the kids to choose from. These can be beginning readers, chapter books, and nonfiction. Put them on a cart so you can wheel them in and out of the room each week.

Some tips to help make your book buddies program successful:

- Check the books out on a staff library card so they are not showing up as available in the library catalog and you can count the circulation.
- Pull two copies if you can so that both the reader and the listener have their own book to follow along. If you have access to only one copy, do not worry. The pair of buddies can share.
- Encourage kids to check out a book they like or use post-it notes to mark the name and the page number the buddies were on so they can pick up where they left off the next week.

Program Structure

Lori's program involved the parents signing up kids for 30 minutes of reading with a volunteer. Part of that 30 minutes also involved reading activities like word searches, crossword puzzles, or phonics games. The volunteers are committed to listening for one and a half hours. Depending on the number of readers signed up, the volunteers might listen to three different readers each time.

At Cuyahoga County Public Library, I structured my book buddies program slightly differently. We would meet for an hour once a week for six weeks over the summer. The first 30 minutes would be the little and big buddies selecting and reading books together. Then the second 30 minutes would be for small and large group reading games. Appendix C offers an example of what a program might look like.

At Your Library

Book Buddies is a fun program for both school and public libraries. It does not have to cost a cent unless you decide to invest in educational games.

Public Library. Decide if you want to work with adults or teens and tweens as your big buddies. If you go with adults, you will need to factor in background checks unless you work with an organization that does that already. Even if you plan to be in the room the whole time, it is still important to have adult library volunteers background checked before they are partnered with a child.

Once you've made that decision and worked out the details, move on to deciding when and how often you will offer the program. As you plan, you will need to consider the availability of the room you will use and what other activities kids are involved in that might compete with your program. We found that kids had more time in the summer, but it did not work as well during the school year. For Lori, it worked well to offer during the school year.

While the parents are not a part of the book buddies program, it is actually a great opportunity to pull them aside to share information about other library services and programs. You can offer tours of the library, show them how to download e-books, and talk about the benefits of parents reading aloud. It is also a great chance to let them know your policy for children obtaining a library card of their very own. It might take a little coercion to get caregivers to attend, but if you offer coffee and cookies, that will probably be enough to get them in the door.

School Library. School librarians can help facilitate classes partnering up so that younger readers can practice their reading skills. You can put together class sets of books for the kids to choose from and even offer up the library as a place to read with your buddy. This will increase the circulation of the books in your library and support your colleagues.

Since the parents are not available during the school day, you can include information about the program in your newsletter or on the school library's website. A list of books that were used is also helpful. Kids may forget the title of the book they were reading and parents can now have access to check. It makes caregivers a part of the program even if they cannot physically be there.

Building Your Readers Advisory Toolbox

You are probably most familiar with your print collection, but you need to give some attention to the alternate formats too.

- Listen to one audiobook a month—it helps to have ones you like to recommend.
- Read an e-book a quarter—practice changing the font size so you can show caregivers. Apps are continually updated. Using the app throughout the year will keep you up-to-date.

- If you have a large print collection of children's titles, take time once a quarter to familiarize yourself with the titles available. It will help you be ready in a pinch to suggest a better format for a child with visual difficulties.
- Start a list of good read aloud books for multiple age levels. Continue to add titles as you come across them.

References

Articles

Iasevoli, Brenda. "Stop Using the Label 'Struggling Reader,' Author Jacqueline Woodson Advises." *Education Week* (blog). February 5, 2018. http://blogs.edweek.org/edweek/curriculum/2018/02/stop_using_the_label_strugglin.html.

McGuire, Maggie. "The Benefits and Pleasures of Listening to Audiobooks." *Raise a Reader* (blog). *Scholastic Parents.* May 15, 2013. https://www.scholastic.com/parents/books-and-reading/raise-a-reader-blog/benefits-and-pleasures-listening-to-audiobooks.html.

Books

Green, John. **Fault in Our Stars.** Waterville, ME: Thorndike Press Large Print, 2012. 363p. out of print. 9781410450012.

Palacio, R. J. **Wonder.** Waterville, ME: Thorndike Press Large Print, 2013. 481p. $19.99. 9781410457417.

Shannon, David. **A Bad Case of Stripes.** New York, NY: The Blue Sky Press, 1998. unpaged. $17.99. 9780590929974.

Interviews

Lay, Laura. In phone interview with the author. March 23, 2018.

Lori. In interview with the author. June 29, 2018.

Webinar

Grice, Michelle, Lisa Joyce, and Sabine McAlpine. "Engaging Reluctant Readers in Your Library." Baker and Taylor: A Follett Company and Thorndike Press. September 21, 2017.

Website

"Orton-Gillingham." Institute for Multi-Sensory Education. Accessed September 16, 2018. https://www.orton-gillingham.com/about-us/orton-gillingham/.

CHAPTER FIVE

My Child Isn't a Reader—Now What?

It may be hard for you to imagine why a child would not want to read—that he or she would not find joy between the pages of a book or would not choose reading as a hobby. As librarians, we have a passion for the written word and we want everyone to share that passion. But sometimes children just don't.

The Apathetic Reader

My definition of an apathetic reader is a child who does not find reading fun. Apathetic readers may test off the charts for reading ability or they may test below grade level. The true test is whether or not they can read independently. If they can, then they just might need some extra time and attention to help them get over the hump and find books that they enjoy.

The caregivers of apathetic readers may be book lovers who cannot understand why their children do not share the same interest. They read to and in front of their children, have books in the house, and they take their children to the library, but it is still an argument to get their children to pick up a book and read. Parents may also be nonreaders themselves but they want their children to take a different path.

Working with apathetic readers can be challenging at times. You may feel like banging your head against the wall when nothing you suggest is right. After spending a half hour making suggestions, you may find the stack of books abandoned on a table. It is important not to take it personally or let your frustrations show, and there are some steps you can take to combat wishy-washy responses.

Empowering the Reader

An important role that librarians play when working with children is giving them a voice in their book selections. Library staff can be the intermediary between the parent and the child when they are at odds over what counts as reading or what books a child should be allowed or want to read. John Scott, a school librarian in Baltimore, approaches this by talking with parents and offering readers advisory help to elevate anxiety related to reading choices. He talks to caregivers about why it is okay for students to read graphic novels or read on a Kindle. To try to combat some of this unease, I use these phrases to try to build a trusting relationship with families.

- You won't hurt my feelings if you don't want to take a book I suggest.
- If a book doesn't sound interesting, you can tell me and we'll keep looking.
- Go ahead and read the book jacket to see if it appeals to you.
- Feel free to take a stack of books home. Read a chapter or two, and if you don't like the book, *you can stop reading.*
- If it is not for school, you get to choose whether you want to read it all the way through or not.
- Come back and let me know what you thought of the books.
- Letting me know what you like and don't like about a book will help me find you the right book.

This is not to say that I do not still find a pile of books left behind, but it does usually open up some dialogue between the librarian and the child. Telling children that they can stop reading a book they do not like always seems to surprise kids because most of their reading life is made up of books they have to read for school, reports, or because their caregiver liked it as a child.

Readers Advisory When No Child Is Present

It is a conundrum for librarians when parents approach them and say their child does not like to read. They want suggestions, but unfortunately, their child is not at the library with them. These caregivers know you are an expert about books and hope you can magically find that one perfect book that will turn their child on to books. If only it were that simple.

When I was in library school, there was a lot of talk about the fact that you need to talk to the child, not the parent, when you perform a reference or readers advisory interview. That you should encourage the parent to bring the child in to be able to provide the best possible help. I agree that having a child in front of you to interact with is the ideal situation. However, turning this parent away with a "come back with your kid" directive is a missed opportunity. Instead, we need to have that conversation with the live body in front of us.

Caregivers know their child's interests and you can still do a reference or readers advisory interview. Try using some of these questions to get to the heart of what this particular reluctant reader likes. Then take a stab at figuring out what the nonpresent child might want. Yes, it will likely be hit or miss, but it is better than doing nothing. Give the caregiver options to take home so that there is a better chance you will make a match between child and book.

Questions for Caregivers

- Sports—Does your child like to play, watch, read stats?
- Scary—Does your child like scary movies?
- Magical, fantasy, science fiction—Does your child have a good imagination? Does he or she like superheroes?
- Realistic or historical—Does your child like learning about other people?
- Mystery—Does your child like to do puzzles or follow clues?
- Nonfiction—What are your child's hobbies?
- What is your child's favorite subject in school?

Example of Parent-Centered Readers Advisory

When I had this conversation with a parent, I started by talking a bit about the child's likes and dislikes with the mother. I learned that her son was into sports but the mother was not interested in any of the sports books I pulled out. She really felt he would like mysteries because she liked mysteries. I was in a catch-22 moment. I really wanted her to take home a Gordon Korman or a Tim Green book, but that was not what the mother wanted. If I continued to push, she might leave with nothing to bring home for her son to try. This was not what I wanted to see happen.

I took a step back and decided to offer her some mystery books, while also encouraging her to take home at least one of the other books I thought just might spark the reading bug. After a few more minutes of discussing and recommending, she left with *The London Eye Mystery* by Siobhan Dowd and *Masterminds* by Gordon Korman. I suggested she give him both books to explore. The interaction ended with the mother pleased with the books she was checking out for her son. A new relationship was developing between her and the library, and with any luck, next time she would bring her son with her.

Readers Advisory When the Child Is Present with a Parent

A typical transaction that I have witnessed and been a part of with families is when the parent announce that his or her child does not like to read—can you please help?—right in front of the child. You can usually see the

Moods > genres

Mood words can be easier than genres, which are a fairly abstract concept for child readers. Most kids tell me they like mysteries, but rarely choose to read them—I suspect they have just more familiarity with a "mystery" compared to other genres. Some of the mood words I use most frequently include:

- Funny
- Hopeful
- Moving
- Quiet
- Quirky
- Sad
- Scary
- Spooky
- Suspenseful
- Upbeat

Figure 5.1 Mood
Reprinted with permission from "Readers Advisory for Kids," by Kyra Nay. Parma, Ohio: School Age Central Blog, Cuyahoga County Public Library, March 2018.

embarrassment or anger on the child's face as the child listens. If the parent then starts talking about what an older sibling who is a reader likes to read, you can quickly have a disaster on your hands.

One way to redirect this conversation is to ask the child about books that might interest him or her. But instead of using genres, try asking what type of mood the child likes from a book. Figure 5.1 provides some mood words to get you started.

Example of Child-Centered Readers Advisory

When a mother, after asking for my help, proceeded to start pulling books of the shelf and saying things like "Your sister liked this one," it was obvious to me that either this daughter had very different tastes or she simply did not want to read what her sister did. This child did not have the gumption to announce like a teen I know did to her older sister. That teen said, "I don't like the same books you do" and then turned back to me for help. As the librarian, you need to be that voice so the actual reader in the readers advisory transaction can end up with books that will be of interest to them.

With my mother-and-daughter duo, I worked to focus my questions on the daughter directly. Using Nay's technique, I asked her if she was in the mood for a funny book or maybe something scary. This showed the mother, without my having to call her out, that her daughter wanted to read books that appealed to her, not what appealed to the mother or sister. After a little back and forth, I realized that what she liked was a realistic story that was moving. I recommended she try W. Bruce Cameron's A Dog's Purpose series and gave her *Bailey's Story*. These books about dogs that do search and rescue or sniff out cancer were just what she was looking for even though they are told from the dog's perspective. Another book I thought she might like was *Three Pennies* by Melanie Crowder. A foster kid is not so sure about being adopted because she is still hoping her mother will come back. My customer left feeling much more confident in her finds, and the mother was happy she had books to check out.

Collection Development and Merchandising: High-Interest Formats

When working with families that have children who are not drawn to books, the format you give them becomes even more important. Simply sharing popular middle grade fiction or beginning readers may not be enough to hook these kids. Instead, you need to dig a little deeper and examine the formats you circulate for their appeal to a more visual or fact-seeking reader.

High-interest books tend to circulate really well so you might not have a lot on your shelves at any one time. This is a problem in some of my branches as the kids do not like to place holds and neither do their parents. When it comes to kid's books, the majority seem to want immediate gratification at least 95 percent of the time.

If the usual response to placing a hold is "I'll just get it next time," you know that you may not have it on that next trip but it can be a challenge to make families understand. A tip for floating collections is to place a hold on a staff card for titles and subjects you are asked for but you do not have in your branch. This way you might just have it when they come back. And if not, you'll probably make someone else super happy.

Beginning Reader Graphic Novels

Books that combine graphic novel elements with beginning reader visuals can help kids take greater strides to becoming fluent readers. I have found that caregivers are not as resistant to graphic novels that are targeted to this younger age group. I think this is because parents understand the importance of illustration to learning to read. These titles will not likely be hard to sell to either the parent or the child.

Currently, I place most of these books in the beginning reader collection. However, as demand rises, along with the number being published, creating a section for graphic novel beginning readers is a direction you can take. If you are ready to create a separate section, I would recommend putting it at either the start or end of the fiction beginning readers rather than with middle grade graphic novels. Here are a few examples of excellent graphic novel readers.

Annable, Graham. **Peter & Ernesto: A Tale of Two Sloths.** New York, NY: First Second, 2018. 119p. (Peter & Ernesto). $17.99. 9781626725614.
Ernesto longs for adventure and leaves the comfort of the tree. Peter, a homebody, must gather his courage and leave the tree too in order to find his friend.

Brunetti, Ivan. **3X4.** New York, NY: Toon Books, 2018. unpaged. $12.95. 9781943145348.
A school assignment has the students drawing sets of items that add up to 12.

Clanton, Ben. **Narwhal: Unicorn of the Sea.** Toronto, ON: Tundra Books, 2016. 64p. (A Narwhal and Jelly Book). $12.99. 9781101918265.
Narwhal makes friends at sea and eats some yummy waffles.

Jamieson, Victoria. **The Great Pet Escape.** New York, NY: Henry Holt and Company, LLC, 2016. 63p. (Pets on the Loose). $15.99. 9781627791052.
The class pets are planning their escape when they come across the school's mice population and their dastardly plot.

Cartoon Beginning Readers

When I visit branches, the echoing refrain I hear is that we need more of these cartoon readers. The kids love them and will flip through what is available to find their favorites. At Cuyahoga County Public Library I purchase paperback cartoon readers. They are cheaper so I can buy lots of copies. I typically purchase 50 to 60 copies of each title for our 28 branches. Rather than shelve these skinny paperbacks spine out, we use Demco's Magboxes.

Magboxes were created for magazines, but they work great for this collection too. The clear acrylic means that kids can see the cover of the first book and will be drawn in by seeing Superman, My Little Pony, Thomas the Tank, Dora the Explorer, or Mickey Mouse. I look for Disney, Lego, Superhero, Star Wars, Nickelodeon, and Netflix television shows when purchasing cartoon beginning readers.

Some publisher lines that release cartoon readers include the following:

- Disney Book Group's World of Reading
- Harper's I Can Read
- DK Publishing's DK Readers
- Little Brown and Company's Passport to Reading

- Random House Children's Books' Step into Reading
- Penguin's Penguin Young Readers

Graphic Novels

You may find some resistance from caregivers about graphic novels for older readers. They may say, "But it is not really reading." Natasha Forrester Campbell from Multnomah County Library lets parents know that reading graphic novels actually requires kids to use both sides of their brain. They have to decipher the words as well as the pictures. This can lead to reading more difficult texts with harder vocabulary simply because the images can help kids decode words. At Rocky River Public Library, Nicole L. Martin talks to parents about how reading a graphic novel can be a confidence booster. It can allow a child to read a much longer (in page-length) book than they would otherwise be capable of. She also sees it as a jumping-off point to other reading formats.

If you are a lover of graphic novels like Martin is, you will want to bring that enthusiasm to the conversation with both the parent and the child. If parents witness your appreciation for the format, they might be more willing to allow their child to read it. Additionally, Forrester Campbell and Martin have noticed that kids who read graphic novels will read them three to five times in a single month before coming to a book discussion. A parent factoid here would be that kids are deeply engaged with a graphic novel and notice new details every time they reread. If they were reading a chapter book, they would likely not be working so closely with the text.

Martin has also seen an increase of graphic novel titles showing up on the school's summer reading lists, and when kids are simply required to read a certain number of books over the summer, graphic novels are allowed to be among those books. Having teacher support definitely translates into more kids asking for graphic novels at the library and provides the perfect opportunity for librarians to show caregivers the wide variety of genres that fall under the format of graphic novel.

Even if you are not a fan of graphic novels personally, you need to read at least a few to become familiar with the format. Reviews can help you expand your recommendation pile but nothing beats reading them yourself.

Brooks, Molly. **Sanity & Tallulah.** New York, NY: Disney Hyperion, 2018. 227p. (Sanity & Tullulah). $12.99pa. 9781368022804pa.
   A science project gone wrong wreaks havoc on a spaceship, and it is up to a child scientist to save the day.
Brosgol, Vera. **Be Prepared.** Illustrated by Vera Brosgol and Alec Longstreth. New York, NY: First Second, 2018. 245p. $12.99pa. 9781626724457pa.
   Loosely based on the author's own childhood, Vera goes to a Russian American summer camp that is not quite what she was hoping for.

Chanani, Nidhi. **Pashmina**. New York, NY: First Second, 2017. 169p. $16.99pa. 9781626720879pa.

A magical pashmina offers Pri insight into her mother's life in India.

Jamieson, Victoria. **Roller Girl**. New York, NY: Dial Books for Young Readers, 2015. 240p. $20.99. 9780525429678.

Roller Derby helps a tween, Astrid, deal with changing friendships.

Martin, Ann M. **Kristy's Great Idea.** Illustrated by Raina Telgemeier and Braden Lamb. New York, NY: Graphix, 2015 (2006). 181p. (The Baby-Sitters Club). $10.99pa. 9780545813877pa.

Characters and stories first introduced in the 1980s have been brought back for a new generation in a new format. Best friends Kristy, Mary Anne, Claudia, and Stacey join forces to provide babysitters for all the neighbors and support each other through middle school.

Pilkey, Dav, and Jose Garibaldi. **Dog Man.** New York, NY: Graphix, 2016. 231p. (Dog Man). $9.99. 9780545581608.

An injured police officer and police dog are stitched together to create a new hero—Dog Man.

Scott, Mairghread. **Robots and Drones: Past, Present, and Future.** Illustrated by Jacob Chabot. New York, NY: First Second, 2018. 121p. (Science Comics). $12.99pa. 9781626727922pa.

Mixing fact and graphic novel format, the evolution of robots is explored.

Sell, Chad, Jay Fuller, David Demeo, Katie Schenkel, Manuel Betancourt, Molly Muldoon, Vid Alliger, Cloud Jacobs, Michael Cole, and Barbara Perez Marquez. **The Cardboard Kingdom.** New York, NY: Alfred A. Knopf, 2018. 281p. $21.99. 9781549039973.

A diverse group of neighborhood kids gather together to create and act out their own fantastical kingdom.

Yang, Gene Luen. **Secret Coders.** Illustrated by Mike Holmes. New York, NY: First Second, 2015. 91p. (Secret Coders). $9.99pa. 9781626720756pa.

Friends must use their computer-programming skills to save their school.

Comic Books

At Cuyahoga County Public Library, we carry comic books for both kids and teens. They are a mixture of superhero titles along with other character-based series. Rather than working with a book vendor, we instead work directly with a local comic book shop. The mother and son owners provide excellent service and help me make sure we have a selection of some of the hottest comics being put out each year.

In the fall, I contact them through e-mail and ask for information on any new titles we should pick up and what series might have concluded. We typically order between 20 and 25 kids titles and 20 to 25 teen titles. With their suggestions, I then do a Survey Monkey poll of the branch staff to see if they want a full set of all titles or a selection of about half the titles. From their responses, I send a spreadsheet to the comic book shop with the titles and quantities we want. This sets up our standing order. After that, once a month the comics are delivered to the library's administrative offices so they can be barcoded and sent out to the branches.

Comics are a good choice for kids looking for a quick read and those who like artwork with their stories. It can also be a way for a parent and a child to connect if the parent was a comic-book reader as a child. The cost for comics is pretty cheap at between $2.99 and $3.99 an issue. As mentioned with graphic novels, comics can be that jumping-off point to other formats once kids find genres that they like reading.

Hybrid Books

Chapter books and middle grade titles that have longer texts but are still heavily illustrated are a growing format in the children's book world. Hybrid books might be more acceptable to caregivers who are leery of graphic novels, and you can steer the conversation in this direction if you are getting nowhere on all the benefits of reading a graphic novel.

Baltazar, Armand. **Diego and the Rangers of the Vastlantic.** New York, NY: Katherine Tegen Books, 2017. 607p. (Timeless). $19.99. 9780062402363.
A post-apocalypse novel where the past, present, and future all exist together. Animation-style illustrations increase the action and suspense.

DiCamillo, Kate. **Flora & Ulysses: The Illuminated Adventures.** Illustrated by K. G. Campbell. Somerville, MA: Candlewick Press, 2013. 233p. $17.99. 9780763660406.
With the help of a little magic and a superhero squirrel, Flora finds a way to stand up for herself. A mix of illustration and comic panels enhance the story.

Libenson, Terri. **Invisible Emmie.** New York, NY: Balzer + Bray, 2017. 185p. $10.99. 9780062484932.
Two girls in middle school have very different experiences. One story is told as a narrative with illustrations, and the other is told through comic panels.

Vernon, Ursula. **Harriet the Invincible.** New York, NY: Dial Books for Young Readers, 2015. 247p. (Hamster Princess). $12.99. 9780803739833.
Harriet is not your typical princess. Rather than waiting for Prince Charming to save the day, she does it herself. Color illustration and speech balloons share the pages of text.

Chapter Book Series

This format is near and dear to my heart. As a kid who took a little longer to learn to read and who was not a confident reader, series books are what made me a bookworm. I read all the original Baby-Sitter's Club books by Ann M. Martin as well as the Sweet Valley Twins series created by Francine Pascal. I discovered these books in my fourth-grade teacher's classroom library, and after that, I became a regular at the public library so I could read and reread all my favorites.

My word of caution to librarians is to not dismiss these books as fluff or lesser reading. We need to remember to be advocates for kids who eat up the books that have similar plots each time and those who have characters they can rely on. It is your job as the keeper of the books to let parents know that it is perfectly normal and acceptable for kids to want to read series. That they will likely move on to other books as they get older, but there is no rush or time table.

If a caregiver is persistent or even a coworker is, I would remind them that many adults like to read their series books or every book by an author. James Patterson, Janet Evanovich, Louise Penny, and John Sandford are just a few examples of these types of authors for adults. Finding a series that a kid loves might just be what turns them into a lifelong reader.

Florence, Debbi Michiko. **Jasmine Toguchi, Mochi Queen.** Illustrated by Elizabet Vukovic. New York, NY: Farrar Straus Giroux, 2017. 115p. (Jasmine Toguchi). $15.99. 9780374304102.
>Jasmine wants to help make mochi, a traditional Japanese New Year food, but must convince her family that she is old enough and strong enough to help.

Kelly, David A. **The Fenway Foul-Up.** Illustrated by Mark Meyers. New York, NY: Random House, 2011. 101p. (Ballpark Mysteries). $4.99pa. 9780375867033pa.
>Cousins figure out who stole the star baseball player's bat.

Meadows, Daisy. **Shelley the Sugar Fairy.** New York, NY: Scholastic Inc., 2017. 65p. (Rainbow Magic: The Sweet Fairies). $4.99pa. 9781338207255pa.
>The Candy Harvest must be saved from the trickster goblin Jack Frost, who has stolen Shelley's magic.

Simon, Coco. **Sunday Sundaes.** New York, NY: Simon Spotlight, 2018. 144p. (Sprinkle Sundays). $6.99pa. 9781534417465pa.
>Starting at a new school and dealing with your parents' recent divorce is not easy, but with the help of friends and ice cream, it is all a little more bearable.

Warner, Sally. **EllRay Jakes Is NOT a Chicken!** Illustrated by Jamie Harper. New York, NY: Viking, 2011. 108p. (EllRay Jakes). $14.99. 9780670062430.
>An African American third-grade boy deals with bullies while anticipating a trip to Disneyland.

Nonfiction

Nonfiction books for reports are necessary to have in your library's collections. They recount the facts of a person, an animal, or a time in history. They can explain how things work and show readers how to attempt an experiment or a recipe themselves, or with the help on an adult. However, the writing style of some nonfiction books can be a little dry. To excite the inquisitive child, you will want to also have books that spark curiosity. Some things to look for include high-quality color photographs, back matter that shows the research the author undertook, and nonfiction titles that read like fiction.

Arnold, Tedd. **Why, Fly Guy?: A Big Question & Answer Book.** New York, NY: Scholastic Inc., 2107. 128p. (Fly Guy Presents). $14.99. 9781338053180.
>   The why questions kids have always wanted the answer to, and answers to questions they have never thought to ask, are answered through a mix of photographs, comic stripes, and snippets of text. It makes this a book that kids can dip in and out of.

Frost, Helen. **Wake Up!** Illustrated by Rick Lieder. Somerville, MA: Candlewick Press, 2017. unpaged. $15.99. 9780763681494.
>   Stunning photographs give a close-up look at nature.

Gigliotti, Jim. **Who Was George Washington Carver?** Illustrated by Stephen Marchesi. New York, NY: Penguin Workshop, 2015. 105p. (Who Was). $5.99pa. 9780448483122pa.
>   A series of chapter book biographies that include illustrations and are written in a narrative style. At right around the 100 pages mark, they work for middle grade reports as well as for those who like reading to learn new things.

Jenkins, Martin. **Bird Builds a Nest.** Illustrated by Richard Jones. Somerville, MA: Candlewick Press, 2018. 26p. (A First Science Storybook). $16.99. 9780763693466.
>   Short sentences and words in a larger font explain the steps birds follow when making their nest. An add-on at the end includes an explanation of the science concepts of pushing and pulling along with ways for kids to practice them.

Osborne, Mary Pope, and Natalie Pope Boyce. **Dragons and Mythical Creatures.** Illustrated by Carlo Molinari. New York, NY: Random House, 2016. 123p. (Magic Tree House Fact Tracker). $12.99. 9781101936375.
>   After reading about Jack and Annie's fictional adventure, kids can pick up the fact tracker to help them separate fact from fiction, like whether unicorns or mermaids are real.

Inviting Parents into Library Programs

Offering fun and engaging programs for preschool and school age kids can help them develop a love of reading and an appreciation for other subjects like math and art. By inviting the parents to participate in your programs, you give families a chance to learn and experience something together.

Family Graphic Novel Book Group—Multnomah County Public Library, Oregon, Hollywood Library

If you are looking for a way to bring the parents and kids together, a book discussion is a great way to do it. By choosing to discuss graphic novels, you are potentially reaching kids who would not come to traditional book discussion of novels. You are also showing parents that graphic novels as a format is a legitimate form of reading. With parents present, they can see their children develop as readers. They will see how well they comprehend the text and art as well as how they mature as discussion participants.

Background

Natasha Forrester Campbell started her first graphic novel book discussion in 2016 because she was looking for a way to help the second and third graders transition out of early readers. Many of these kids were not quite ready for chapter books but were beyond the traditional beginning readers. Forrester Campbell saw graphic novels as a great way to bridge the two, and from the start, she included parents. When the typical book discussion for fourth and fifth graders started to dwindle in attendance, she also transitioned it to a graphic novel book discussion with the parents participating.

The Program

Forrester Campbell's program is similar in many ways to a traditional book discussion. In Appendix D, an outline of one of her discussions is included. Just like with other book discussions, you need to read the books before deciding if they will make a good book discussion title for your library. Also, if you are going to offer a graphic novel book discussion, the presenter should enjoy and be enthusiastic about the graphic novel format. If that is not you, that is okay, but find the person at your library who is.

When selecting titles, she likes to include a variety of genres, including nonfiction. She also looks for books that show inclusive experiences, cultures, and social perspectives. She finds that parents tend to notice and are happy about it. To make families a part of the process, Forrester Campbell has them help choose the titles that will be discussed. She usually book talks about 12 to 14 titles at the first meeting of the year in October. She has two to four titles that she absolutely wants to discuss and then lets the families pick the other titles. An added side benefit is that many of the kids will decide to read the other titles not selected.

The Discussion. She has general questions that she can use for any graphic novel. She also creates questions that are specific to the graphic novel being discussed. Everyone is expected to participate in the discussion, including the parents. Most times the parents will give the kids the chance to speak first. However, Forrester Campbell makes sure the adults also share their thoughts and opinions. This makes for a richer discussion for all.

Another piece that stems from having the parents reading the same book is that families are encouraged to talk about the book before they attend the discussion. They do not have to wait to share the excitement they are feeling, ask each other questions, or express disappointment in a part of the story or artwork that they did not like. She finds everyone still has plenty to say to the group as a whole, but prediscussion allows for the parents to gauge the amount of the story their child has comprehended on his or her own.

The Activity. After discussion, there is an extension activity that connects back to the graphic novel. It can be art based or narrative based. It can be a game or something more tactile. It will really just depend on the book you choose and how it inspires you.

The Snack. Even the snack is linked to the book being discussed. It has become a game of guess the connection among the kids. The cost of the program is pretty minimal and could be made to fit any budget. Forrester Campbell spends around $10 to $20 each month for the activities supplies and the snacks.

Logistics

Family Graphic Novel Book Group is offered once a month from October to June. Forrester Campbell offers it on Sunday afternoons. The second- and third-grade group meets first, and then later that day is the gathering of the fourth- and fifth-grade group. She finds that parents with siblings in both age groups will sometime split up, and other times, the same parent will attend both discussions. Families attending find the program valuable and will make the time to come each month. On average, Forrester Campbell sees 12 to 22 participants at the younger group and 10 to 14 at the older group.

Advertising

Most libraries face some competition for a kid's after-school time. There are many activities that kids participate in such as sports, dance, theater, and music. To keep interest up, a postcard-size flyer is placed in graphic novel titles. A flyer is also displayed on the shelves in the graphic novel section.

At the start of the school year, Forrester Campbell drops off flyers so that one can go in each teacher's mailbox. She will also e-mail or stop by and chat with teachers about the book discussion. She does find that one of the best ways to get new families is by word of mouth between parents. Other avenues used are the library's website and event calendar. Word of mouth also comes from the library staff who will invite families they see browsing by the graphic novel section.

Implementing

As you decide if a graphic novel book discussion is right for your library, I would look at two key elements: your circulation statistics for the format and how often you see kids browsing the section. If you find that the interest is there, go for it!

Public Library. You may have to play around with the day and time to find one that works for your families. In my library system, Sundays are usually a little lighter on staff and we are only open from 1:00 P.M. to 5:00 P.M. so it would probably not work. Some branches find that right after school or right after dinner is the best time. If you want to do one that is more for home-school families, you could consider offering it during the day.

Depending on the size and setup of your library, either you will need to earmark some of your budget for the books or you will need to talk to your collection development staff about purchasing those copies for you. In some cases, you will be able to call in copies from multiple branches in your system or work with your consortium to acquire the copies needed.

The activities you choose and whether you offer a snack may need to be tied into the budget you have. You can make them very simple and therefore not expensive. If you would like to be more elaborate, an option might be to ask your Friends of the Library for a small program budget. Remember Forrester Campbell only spends $10 to $20 a month.

School Library. If you want to try a graphic novel book discussion, a good time to have it would be during lunch. Kids will bring their lunch, and then you do not have to worry about budgeting for a snack. You will either need to budget money to purchase copies of the titles for the discussion or see if you can get sufficient copies from your public library. Parent–teacher groups might be able to help or profits from a Scholastic or Follett Book Fair might be used too.

In most cases, you probably will not be able to make it a parent–child discussion. If you think you can get caregivers, I would give it a go. If not, consider having an end-of-year discussion and celebration and invite the caregivers to it. It might be easier for them to only have to take off work one time, and it would still give them a chance to see what a graphic novel discussion looks like.

Depending on the length of the lunch period, you can do a discussion of the book and still have time for an activity. If time is short, you can simply do the discussion but you might consider getting a button maker and giving the kids a button each time that relates to the book. You will likely get participants who were on the fence about participating decide to come back to get that next button.

Evaluating Your Program

Your first clue of success will be the willingness of the caregivers to not only attend but also take the time to read the graphic novel ahead of time. Forrester Campbell has heard things like "My child hates nonfiction and will not read it, but she will read graphic novel nonfiction like the Science Comics series." It is a true joy to help kids find the books that inspire them to read more.

Predicting the Caldecott Winner—Dayton Metro Library, Ohio, Wilmington-Stroop Branch Library

Visual learners will have a chance to shine at programs that focus on art. This can be the study of famous artists and the creation of art that is in a similar style. It can also be an appreciation and study of the art techniques used to illustrate children's books. Recognizing that kids learn differently and offering programs that support visual literacy can help parents appreciate the fact that their kids are multitalented.

Background

After attending the Dayton Metro Library's Mock Caldecott program for librarians, Melissa Sokol thought her families would like to give selecting a winner and honor books a try. With a regular Tuesday night Family Storytime, she had a built-in audience for the program. Working at a suburban library branch, she is lucky to have parents who continually bring their kids, ranging in age from 2 to 12 years old, to library programs.

Planning

Sokol worked with a children's librarian at another branch who was on the Dayton Mock Caldecott Committee. They looked at Jen J's spreadsheet of starred reviews for titles to consider. From there the list was narrowed down to titles that kids would like. Although not on the list of criteria for the real committee, it was an important one for this program. Sokol then compared her list to the library's holdings to see which titles had copies available.

This narrowed things down to 20 titles, and for a couple of them, like *Grand Canyon* illustrations and text by Jason Chin, she talked with her collection development department about getting a few extra copies since all currently owned copies were checked out. Her goal was to have two copies of each title available for participants to look at during the program.

Since the focus of the Caldecott is the artwork and how it tells the story, Sokol contacted a local high school art teacher who happened to be studying for his master's in fine arts. By lucky happenstance, she knew his wife, a former Dayton librarian and current school librarian at the high school. Having someone with an art background in the room helped to elevate the discussion surrounding medium and technique used in the illustrations.

Budget

The budget for the program was pretty minimal, which is nice for libraries with limited finances. Sokol did provide snacks, as the program went on for one and a half hours, 6:30 P.M.–8:00 P.M., on a week night. She thought ahead of the fact that some caregivers might not have time for a real dinner before coming to the program. The inclusion of snacks reminded me of a real Caldecott Committee tradition, where members often bring a snack from their home state to share during the long days of discussion at the American Library Association's Midwinter Conference.

The art teacher did offer his time free of charge, so there was no upfront cost. To show her appreciation and thanks, Sokol did purchase a fun library-related tee shirt and a box of chocolate for him. Along with that, she provided a deposit collection of books being used for the Predicting the Caldecott Winner program for use with his high school art students. This happened about a month before the library program and allowed for a second, unofficial study of the books.

Advertising

Deciding on a title for the program was carefully thought out. Having the right catchy title can make the difference in how many people click on the event link to find out more information. Traditionally, programs like Sokol's might be called a "Mock Caldecott." Instead of using this title for her program, she went with the title "Predicting the Caldecott Winner" because she felt it would resonate better with her families.

Then came deciding when would be the best time to offer the program to garner the most participation from families. Sokol decided to offer it the same night as her Family Storytime. Weekly storytimes go on hiatus at the end of November and the first week of December during that Family Storytime slot is an annual puppet show. To keep the momentum going, she decided to host the "Predicting the Caldecott Winner" the second week of December.

Once the title and date were chosen, she then turned to getting the word out. There was no budget for flyers, so the program was primarily advertised on the library's online event calendar. As this is where all library programs can be located, it did get some automatic traffic. The most effective way of getting the word out turned out to be word of mouth via Sokol. She talked it up to her regular families as a big read-in that would be super fun. All of the forethought put into naming, picking a date, and advertising paid off as she had 27 participants the first time she offered the program in 2017.

Parent Engagement and Literacy

The program focus was reading the books through their illustrations as the Caldecott Award focuses on the artwork rather than the words. This meant that even the youngest child could view the book without needing a lot of help. However, parents were encouraged to experience the books with their children, and having an art teacher present allowed for him to help facilitate this. He could go around the room and talk with families about the medium used in the book and let the kids and parents know that a style of artwork like *Big Cat, Little Cat* was deceptively simple and actually very difficult to create.

When talking about literacy, caregivers may have tunnel vision and only be thinking about reading, reading levels, and fluency as a reader. What Sokol was able to do with this art program was to show caregivers that literacy is broader than the written word and that interpreting art is also an acquired and important skill that needs to be developed over time. Visual storytelling actually helps level the playing field and allows a less strong reader to stand out for his or her knowledge set. This is a great thing for the child to experience and the parent to witness.

Program Structure

The Predicting the Caldecott Winner program started off with some content that was targeted to the parents and older kids. This introductory piece included things like:

- Sharing previous Caldecott winners that the attendees might be familiar with.
- Talking about the Caldecott Committee make-up of 15 participants who are either elected or appointed.

- That committee participants must be members of the American Library Association and the Association for Library Service to Children in order to be eligible to serve.
- What the criteria for the award is.
- How the Caldecott Medal is a prestigious award and that there is no monetary gain for the committee members.
- Things to concentrate on when viewing a book are end papers, secret covers like in *Mr. Tiger Goes Wild*, and gutter issues.

From here, Sokol gave the participants a sheet with each title listed and asked them to rank each book they viewed from 1 to 10 so they would remember what they thought about each book by the end of the night. An example of the sheet can be found in Appendix E. After viewing the books, the kids then were given the chance to vote on their top-three picks, just like the real Caldecott Committee. She tallied the votes on a white board with the back to the kids. This built up anticipation and many kids tried to peek around the side to see what was getting the most votes.

Once tallied, it was announced that there was not a clear winner and honor books per the award criteria. The list was then narrowed down to the eight most voted for titles. The group briefly discussed all eight titles as a group to see what stood out about them, both the good and the bad. Then a second vote was taken, and there was a clear winner and honor book.

Winner. **The Legend of Rock Paper Scissors** illustrated by Adam Rex

Honor. **Big Cat, Little Cat** illustrated by Elisha Cooper

Response from Families

One of the most memorable moments came from a two-year-old. This little girl impressed everyone when she was able to tell the story of *Big Cat, Little Cat* just by looking at the images. Her interpretation was the (white) cat was coming back versus it being a new cat. Perfectly reasonable storytelling for one so young. This truly showcased why the program could work with a broad range of ages.

For Next Time

Looking to the future, there are some things that she would improve upon. For example, she would be a little more purposeful in using the art teacher's expertise and would introduce each book and what type of art or medium was used in its creation. She would also like to add a storytime after the awards announcement. This would allow her to share the Caldecott Committee's winner and honor books and discuss with participants what they think about the choices.

Another great idea for larger libraries would be to create a rotating kit of titles that can be shared with other branches so more librarians could offer the program. This would entail working with the collection development staff, or whoever handles book ordering, to get extra copies of the chosen titles to be placed in the kit. The added advantage would be knowing you had all the titles you needed without the challenge of calling them in. If this is not an option for you because of lack of funding or space to house, you could also work with interlibrary loan to secure the additional copies you need.

Extending the Program—Public and School Libraries

Here are some ways that I think you could easily market this program beyond hosting a mock or predicting the award program in a public library setting. One way would be for school librarians to adopt this program since they have direct access to art teachers. Another possibility would be the public library, school library, and an art teacher teaming up together. The program's mock night could be held at the school and then a follow-up storytime after the real announcement could be held at the public library. Developing this partnership is a win-win for schools and public libraries as it offers both institutions a chance to engage with families in a fun and educational way.

Math Olympiad—Santa Clara City Library, California, Northside Branch Library

Literacy does not just mean being able to read a street sign or a novel. There are all kinds of ways to be literate, and for some kids, math is their forte. They enjoy solving problems that involve both numbers and letters. When libraries offer programs that dig into the nonfiction side of the collection, they open the doors to families who might not otherwise come through the doors.

Background

At her current and previous libraries, Cheryl Lee had parents who are very active in their children's education and who are looking for additional enrichment for their kids. While at Palo Alto City Library, Lee became familiar with Communication Academy, an organization that was already offering Math Olympiad programs at the recreation center. But those programs required paying a fee, and the library could offer them to families at no charge. She first offered them in Palo Alto, and now she offers them at the Santa Clara City Library's Northside Branch Library.

The Program

Math Olympiad is a national program that encourages a love for math in fourth through eighth graders and offers tournaments for individual and team competition. To participate you have to be part of a school team. Northside's program is slightly different. Kids in second and third grade attend one session and kids in fourth through sixth grade attend a separate session. The program is not part of the official Math Olympiad tournaments but, instead, gives parents and kids a taste of what Math Olympiad is all about.

Kids are given old questions from previous Math Olympiad test years, and they work to solve them either individually or as part of a team. Then the instructor calls the group back together to discover what the correct answer is and to have the kids explain how they got the answer. Structuring the session in this way gets the competitive juices flowing and quickly engrosses the kids in the solving of each problem.

Parent Involvement

Parents are invited to attend the program with their child but are asked not to bring siblings with them. Younger brothers and sisters tend to be distracting to the participants. When the parents do come in, the instructors will ask them to try solving the same problems as the kids. It then becomes a learning experience for all, especially if the kids get it right and the adults do not.

Feedback from parents has been really positive, including asking things like "when will it be offered again" and "how come no other library offers it." Another sign that the program is meeting a family need is that people come from outside the community, some traveling 20 to 30 minutes just to attend.

Advertising

After presenting Math Olympiad for four years, Northside does not have to do a lot of promotion to have the program fill up and to have a waiting list. Registration opens up 30 days before the program date and a reminder e-mail to caregivers is sent the day of the program.

Typically, the program is listed on Eventbrite, the software they use for online registration. It tends to sell itself and the parents spread the word by word of mouth. Occasionally, Lee will share on the library's Facebook page if registration is not as brisk as usual.

Tips from the Trenches

Math programs can work for both public and school libraries. They likely will be an unexpected surprise for families who only think of the library as a place to check out books or to attend storytime. Getting the word out that you are providing math literacy programs just might bring in new families to your library.

Public Library. It is important to listen to your community and offer programs that caregivers are asking for. By listening, you can start to meet and even exceed the expectations of the parents. One key thing to look at is when to hold a program. After school on Wednesdays work best for Northside as that is a shorter school day for the public schools. The teachers have staff meetings so the kids get out of school about an hour early. This works for the public school parents, and as long as the program is not offered too early, it also works for the private school families. To help with accessible times, the program is also offered on Saturday mornings so that working parents or kids with after-school activities can still have an opportunity to come.

School Library. If you are able to partner with a teacher, you could offer a math challenge program during lunch and recess or as an after-school club. You would need to check with your building principal and teachers to see when other clubs are offered. Another option is to partner with some math teachers and provide additional math resources for students who need to be challenged or offer your own math competition night in the school library and invite caregivers to come and see firsthand the skills of their child. With the focus on STEM in schools, you are likely to be embraced by colleagues as a team player and you will be showing an added benefit of the school library and school librarian.

Making It Happen

Lee estimates that Northside Branch Library spends approximately $1,000 to offer Math Olympiad four to six times a year. The program is funded by grants from the Santa Clara City Foundation & Friends. With attendance maxing out at 25 kids and the fact that they reach that number each time the program is offered, she finds that it is money well spent.

This up-front cost might be a challenge for some libraries, but hosting a math competition program can also be done at a lower cost. You might have someone at your library with an affinity for math who would love to take on the challenge of creating a math competition program and the problems to go with it. If that is not the case, this would be a great opportunity to partner with a math teacher and develop a connection between the public library and a local school or between the school librarian and a fellow teacher. If you can get volunteer help to create the math problems, your program cost would then just be for supplies like paper and pencils.

Building Your Readers Advisory Toolbox

Seek out highly illustrated books for readers of all ages.

• Read at least four graphic novels per year (mix of beginning reader and chapter books).
• Read at least three books that are the first book in a new series per year.
• Read three hybrid books each year.
• Visit a local comic book shop once a year and check out what the most popular titles are.

References

Books

Brown, Peter. **Mr. Tiger Goes Wild.** New York, NY: Little Brown and Company, 2013. unpaged. $18.00. 9780316200639.

Cameron, W. Bruce. **Bailey's Story.** Illustrated by Richard Cowdrey. New York, NY: A Tom Doherty Associates Book, 2016. 206p. (A Dog's Purpose Novel). $16.99. 9780765388407.

Chin, Jason. **Grand Canyon.** New York, NY: A Neal Porter Book, 2017. unpaged. $19.99. 9781596439504.

Cooper, Elisha. **Big Cat, Little Cat.** New York, NY: Roaring Brook Press, 2017. unpaged. $16.99. 9781626723719.

Crowder, Melanie. **Three Pennies.** New York, NY: Atheneum Books for Young Readers, 2017. 181p. $16.99. 9781481471879.

Daywalt, Drew. **The Legend of Rock Paper Scissors.** Illustrated by Adam Rex. New York, NY: Balzer + Bray, 2017. unpaged. $17.99. 9780062438898.

Dowd, Siobhan. **The London Eye Mystery.** New York, NY: David Fickling Books, 2007. 323p. $15.99. 9780375849763.

Korman, Gordon. **Masterminds.** New York, NY: Balzer + Bray, 2015. 321p. (Masterminds). $16.99. 9780062299963.

Interviews

Forrester Campbell, Natasha. In online interview with the author. August 2, 2018.

Lee, Cheryl. In phone interview with the author. August 28, 2018.

Martin, Nicole L. In interview with the author. August 2, 2018.

Scott, John. In e-mail interview with the author. August 30, 2017.

Sokol, Melissa. In phone interview with the author. April 9, 2018.

Websites

"Build Better Math Students through Contests!" Math Olympiad for Elementary and Middle Schools. Accessed September 16, 2018. https://www.moems .org.

"Magbox." Demco. Accessed September 17, 2018. https://www.demco.com/ goto?magbox2.

"Starred Reviews." Jen J's Booksheets: Where Children's/YA Literature and Spreadsheets Collide. Accessed September 17, 2018. https://booksheets .wordpress.com/starred-reviews/.

"Welcome to the Caldecott Medal Home Page!" Association for Library Service to Children. Accessed September 17, 2018. http://www.ala.org/alsc/awards grants/bookmedia/caldecottmedal/caldecottmedal.

CHAPTER SIX

Parents of School Age Children, the Library Is Still Here for You!

Literacy is not just the act of learning the alphabet and discovering how the letters make words. Literacy is the foundation for all types of learning. You need literacy to read, to write, to perform science experiments, and even when writing code for a computer program. That is why it is so important to give caregivers the support and tools needed to build that strong foundation in literacy for their children. On the road to independent reading, there can be some bumps in the road, but even once the road starts to smooth out, there is still room for parents and libraries to help a child grow. Library programs offer an extension of what children are learning at school and continue to build a groundwork of literacy that will serve them well as they move to middle school, high school, and even college.

But, as children enter school, the number of activities they are in grows exponentially. Activities such as team sports, music and dance lessons, art classes, and coding clubs all vie for a child's attention and a parent's time. Even caregivers who were regular library users during the toddler and preschool years may not think about the library as a place for after-school enrichment. With lots of competition out there, libraries have had to up their game to show their continued relevance.

How to Get Parents on Board for Enjoyable Reading

The school age years are a time of learning and with that comes homework. Homework can come in different formats such as worksheets, book reports, or research projects. Completing these assignments may feel like a chore for both the parent and the child. The idea of fun, joyful reading like that which was shared during snuggle time as a preschooler can fall by the wayside as school encroaches. While libraries cannot overrule the need to do homework, they can work with families to make sure free-choice reading is still happening.

The Right Book for the Assignment

Once assigned reading starts, families will begin coming to the library with specific types of books they need, usually needed as soon as possible, aka the next day. It is things like "I need a fantasy book" or "I have to do a report on the *Titanic*."

Unfortunately, many times genre or subject reports are not an area of interest for the particular student in front of you. You can usually tell immediately from one's body language and tone of voice. The mother or the father might just be trying to get the books needed and move on to the next item on their to-do list. Or, as I've seen happen, the parents are super excited about the topic but the student is not. When this happens, a child can start to equate reading as work and not a fun pastime.

When it does happen, here is what you can do to help make both the parent and the child a repeat customer. In this example, the genre assigned is historical fiction. To start, I ask for assignment parameters. A question like, "Does it have to be from a particular time in history?" can start to narrow things down. For example, does it need to take place during World War II, the American Revolution, September 11, or the Civil War? If the answer is yes to any of these areas of history, that helps narrow things down a little. If it is no, then the pool of books to recommend from is much larger. From here, I ask what the child likes to read. Past books, even if they are not historical fiction, can help me narrow down to a book I think the child will like. So, if they say they like sports I may suggest a Dan Gutman sports novel like *Willie and Me: A Baseball Card Adventure* as long as the time period doesn't matter.

Adding on a Just-for-Fun Pick

Combat the phenomenon of the boring school assignment reading with this tip that is extremely simple and will cost you nothing! It is a quick add-on to the readers advisory interview. While finding out what a child has to read, the librarian also finds out a little bit about what he or she likes to read or do. Then, once you have found the book for the report, you can suggest adding on an extra item just for fun.

The child goes home not only with the requisite book for his or her report but also with a book that speaks to him or her. It can be a sports biography, a graphic novel, or a book on World War II. The add-on book can be one that the parent and the child read together, or it can be a book that the child turns to once homework is done for the night. If done successfully, you have both a happy reader and a happy parent leaving your library.

Readers Advisory Straight from the Stacks

I had the pleasure of going back to working in a public library branch for a couple of months in 2018 when the children's librarian went on leave. The Beachwood Branch of Cuyahoga County Public Library is a busy branch and the customers are voracious readers. When I started, I was told that kids come in asking for new series to read and that these kids would then take the whole series that is recommended home with them. It was a cool phenomenon that I experienced myself a few times.

Working with the Above-Average Reader and Parent

One of my favorite readers advisory moments took place with a second-grade boy. The mother was very proud of her son, the reader, and she made sure to let me know that he was reading on a seventh-grade level. When I met him, it was spring break and he needed a few new books to take home. I was called upon to help with the selection of titles. We had a great time talking books and what he liked to read. Not surprising, he loved hybrid books like the Diary of a Wimpy Kid and Captain Underpants series. Many of my first suggestions he had already read. This posed a challenge but also helped me get to know him as a reader.

The mother did interject at one point and apologized to me because his voracious reading habits made recommendations harder. I quickly responded that helping readers find books of interest was my job and was the part I liked the most. It was fun for me to have to dig a little deeper into my own reading history to find just the right books for him. I wanted to make sure both the mother and the son realized that they were not a problem for me and that I was not in a hurry to finish.

I continued making recommendations and discovered that he was not a fan of Star Wars when he turned down Tom Angleberger's Origami Yoda series. Then I struck gold with the following: Mac Barnett's Terrible Two and The Brixton Brothers series as well as The Odd Squad series by Michael Fry. He was super excited to give them a try. He also took an Albert Einstein biography home for a school project.

While many caregivers will insert themselves into the conversation, I was able to respond to the mother's reading-level information and calm her fear that I did have plenty of time to spend helping her son. Other than that, the transaction was mostly between me and the child and the mother hung back. This let him be confident in his reading tastes, and boy was he!

The Reader Who Has Trouble Communicating

A 10-year-old girl came to me asking for help finding something new to read. When I asked what she likes to read, she told me that she likes reading mysteries. I suggested a couple of different mysteries and the mother thought they looked good, but her daughter was not so sure. As we talked further and I asked her what books she had read and liked. She pointed out Lauren Myracle's Flower Power series on the shelf and then said that what she liked was *real* stuff.

That was the turning point of the interaction. I now realized she liked to read books with characters like her or at least books with realistic friendship plots. From there I went on to suggest *Anastasia Krupnik* by Lois Lowry, which is a classic but piqued her interested when I mentioned that Anastasia was dealing with losing her place as an only child. She took the first two books in the series to try.

Collection Development and Merchandising: School Age

A school age collection is going to be made up of a variety of materials to interest children of a wide age span. When you are making reading recommendations or looking for books to use in programs, you are going to be shopping your picture books, beginning reader, fiction, and nonfiction collections. Chapters 1 through 3 offer picture book and beginning reader titles for listeners and early readers, so this chapter will focus on picture books, fiction, and nonfiction titles for older elementary and middle grade readers.

Nonfiction

Since 2010 many states have adopted the Common Core Standards of Education, and these standards place a bigger emphasis on nonfiction. The good news is that there are now a lot of great nonfiction books being published each year. Amazing artwork and photographs are being used to augment the sharing of facts, and the text is written in a narrative style that is more engaging. These books teach but do so in an appealing way that draws kids in. Once kids find a topic they like, the world of nonfiction books opens up to them and they have lots of choices to pick from.

Art

Munro, Roxie. **Masterpiece Mix.** New York, NY: Holiday House, 2017. unpaged. $16.95. 9780823436996.

A brief overview of art techniques and subjects with examples of real paintings woven into the illustrations.

Wallace, Sandra Neil. **Between the Lines: How Ernie Barnes Went from the Football Field to the Art Gallery.** Illustrated by Bryan Collier. New York, NY: A Paula Wiseman Book, 2018. unpaged. $17.99. 9781481443876.

Ernie's passion for the arts is postponed when the opportunity to play professional football presents itself.

Biography

Cline-Ransome, Lesa. **Before She Was Harriet: The Story of Harriet Tubman.** Illustrated by James E. Ransome. New York, NY: Holiday House, 2017. unpaged. $17.95. 9780823420476.

A unique biography that starts at the end of the subject's life and works its way backward.

Bolden, Tonya. **No Small Potatoes: Junius G. Groves and His Kingdom in Kansas.** Illustrated by Don Tate. New York, NY: Alfred A. Knopf, 2018. unpaged. $17.99. 9780385752763.

The story of a former slave who moves to Kansas in the 1880s. By planting potatoes he becomes one of the richest men in the state.

Harvey, Jeanne Walker. **Maya Lin: Artist-Architect of Light and Lines: Designer of the Vietnam Veterans Memorial.** Illustrated by Dow Phumiruk. New York, NY: Christy Ottaviano Books, 2017. unpaged. $17.99. 9781250112491.

Discover the girl who became the woman who entered a contest and won the right to design the Vietnam Veterans Memorial.

Sotomayor, Sonia. **Turning Pages: My Life Story.** Illustrated by Lulu Delacre. New York, NY: Philomel Books, 2018. unpaged. $17.99. 9780525514084.

The first Latina Supreme Court Justice writes her autobiography and shares how books prepared her for her choice in career.

History

Bruchac, Joseph. **Chester Nez and the Unbreakable Code: A Navajo Code Talker's Story.** Illustrated by Liza Amini-Holmes. Chicago, IL: Albert Whitman & Company, 2018. unpaged. $16.99. 9780807500071.

During World War II, men from the Navajo tribe were recruited by the marines to turn their language into a code that the Japanese enemies would not be able to break.

Eggers, Dave. **Her Right Foot.** Illustrated by Shawn Harris. San Francisco, CA: Chronicle Books, 2017. unpaged. $19.99. 9781452162812.

The story of how the Statue of Liberty came to be, what she stands for, and why her right foot is ready to move forward.

Grimes, Nikki. **One Last Word: Wisdom from the Harlem Renaissance.** Illustrated by Cozbi A. Cabrera, R. Gregory Christie, Pat Cummings, Jan Spivey Gilchrist, Ebony Glenn, E. B. Lewis, Frank Morrison, Christopher Myers, Brian Pinkney, Sean Qualls, James Ransome, Javaka Steptoe, Shadra Strickland, and Elizabeth Zunon. New York, NY: Bloomsbury, 2017. 120p. $18.99. 9781619635548.

A tribute to the artists of the Harlem Renaissance. Grimes uses the poetic form called the Golden Shovel. She takes a short poem or a line from a longer poem and then writes her own with the word at the end of each line being one from the original poem. Her poem and the inspiration poem are side by side on the page.

Math

Adler, David A. **Money Math: Addition and Subtraction.** Illustrated by Edward Miller. New York, NY: Holiday House, 2017. 31p. $17.95. 9780823436989.

Just as the title states, this book is about using money as a way to practice adding and subtracting.

Wilding, Karen. **Visual Guide to Math.** New York, NY: DK, 2018. 128p. $16.99. 9781465470935.

When caregivers need a resource to help their elementary school student with math, give them this book. It breaks down over 100 different math terms and uses visuals to help with understanding the concepts.

Poetry

Alexander, Kwame, Chris Colderley, and Marjory Wentworth. **Out of Wonder: Poems Celebrating Poets.** Illustrated by Ekua Holmes. Somerville, MA: Candlewick Press, 2017. 49p. $16.99. 9780763680947.

Each poem tells the story of a well-known poet, and Holmes creates illustrations using different techniques and styles so that they capture the spirit of the poet being recognized.

Harris, Chris. **I'm Just No Good at Rhyming and Other Nonsense for Mischievous Kids and Immature Grown-Ups.** Illustrated by Lane Smith. New York, NY: Little, Brown and Company, 2017. 221p. $19.99. 9780316266574.

In the vein of Shel Silverstein and Jack Prelutsky, these poems are funny, absurd, and just right to read aloud together.

Latham, Irene, Charles Waters, and Sean Qualls. **Can I Touch Your Hair?: Poems of Race, Mistakes, and Friendship.** Illustrated by Selina Alko. Minneapolis, MN: Carolrhoda Books, 2018. 39p. $17.99. 9781512404425.

A black boy and a white girl navigate friendship as they learn about the different experiences they've had because of their race.

Mora, Pat. **Bookjoy, Wordjoy.** Illustrated by Raul Colón. New York, NY: Lee & Low Books Inc., 2018. unpaged. $18.95. 9781620142868.
Celebrate a love of words and poetry and the books that they help create.

Science

Chin, Jason. **Grand Canyon.** New York, NY: A Neal Porter Book, 2017. unpaged. $19.99. 9781596439504.
Discover the Grand Canyon of both the past and present as a father and daughter explore it.

Connolly, Sean. **Book of Wildly Spectacular Sports Science: 60 Hands-On Experiments from Baseball Ballistics to Karate Kinetics.** New York. NY: Workman Publishing, 2016. 243p. $14.95. 9780761189282.
From judo to Frisbee to track and field, the mechanics of sports are broken down into testable feats that kids can test using household supplies and with the help of an adult.

Montgomery, Sy, and Nic Bishop. **The Hyena Scientist.** Boston, MA: Houghton Mifflin Harcourt, 2018. 71p. (Scientists in the Field). $18.99. 9780544635111.
Each book in the series is filled with close-up photographs, and this time it is hyenas. The author shares the most current information about the subject directly from the researchers doing the work.

Technology

Engle, Margarita. **The Flying Girl: How Aida de Acosta Learned to Soar.** Illustrated by Sara Palacios. New York, NY: Atheneum Books for Young Readers, 2018. unpaged. $17.99. 9781481445023.
When hot-air balloons were relatively new, Aida de Acosta pushed the gender boundaries to not only ride in a balloon but also to pilot.

Stone, Tanya Lee. **Who Says Women Can't Be Computer Programmers?: The Story of Ada Lovelace.** Illustrated by Marjorie Priceman. New York, NY: Christy Ottaviano Books, 2018. unpaged. $18.99. 9781627792998.
A short biography on the life of Ada Lovelace, daughter of poet Lord Byron. It was unusual in the nineteenth century for a women's mathematical and imaginative mind to be encouraged but Lovelace's was. She helped create the blueprint for what computers would become a hundred years later.

Fiction

A just-for-fun book can be any book in your collection. The definition of a fun book simply depends on the child you are currently working with. Here are some titles on a variety of themes.

Anderson, John David. **Ms. Bixby's Last Day.** New York, NY: Walden Pond Press, 2016. 300p. $16.99. 9780062338174.

A group of boys in Ms. Bixby's class want the chance to prove how much she means to them so they skip school and travel across town to find her—with a few bumps along the way. (Novel)

Birdsall, Jeanne. **A Summer Tale of Four Sisters, Two Rabbits, and a Very Interesting Boy.** New York, NY: Alfred A. Knopf, 2005. 262p. (The Penderwicks). $15.99. 9780375831430.

A timeless tale of sisterly adventure. (Novel)

Bowles, David. **They Call Me Güero: A Border Kid's Poems.** El Paso, TX: Cinco Puntos Press, 2018. 111p. $18.95. 9781947627062.

Follow the story of Güero, a middle school mexicano boy, who is living in Texas right on the border with Mexico. He is a nerd with a small circle of friends and a girl who just might like him back. (Novel)

Burgos, Hilda Eunice. **Ana María Reyes Does Not Live in a Castle.** New York, NY: Tu Books, 2018. 284p. $18.95. 9781620143629.

Being a middle child in a large family is a tough position to be in. Ana María is a talented piano player and excellent at school. She just needs to find a way to shine within her family. (Novel)

Cartaya, Pablo. **The Epic Fail of Arturo Zamora.** New York, NY: Viking, 2017. 236p. $16.99. 9781101997239.

The family restaurant, La Cocina, is being threatened by a developer so Arturo teams up with his crush, Carmen, to fight back. (Novel)

Child, Brenda J. **Bowwow Powwow: Bagosenjie-niimi'idim.** Translated by Gordon Jourdain. Illustrated by Jonathan Thunder. Saint Paul, MN: Minnesota Historical Society Press, 2018. unpaged. $16.95. 9781681 340777.

Windy Girl loves attending the powwow and listening to the stories of her Ojibwa tribe. Then she starts imagining her own stories. (Picture Book)

Engle, Margarita. **All the Way to Havana.** Illustrated by Mike Curato. New York, NY: Godwin Books, 2017. unpaged. $17.99. 9781627796422.

Take a journey through Cuba in one family's old car and immerse yourself in all the island has to offer. (Picture Book)

Grabenstein, Chris. **Escape from Mr. Lemoncello's Library.** New York, NY: Yearling, 2013. 290p. (Mr. Lemonceollo's Library). $17.99. 97803758 70897.

Smart kids are invited to spend the night at the new library, and if they can solve the mysterious clues left by the building's designer, they win the prize. But this library is not like any library you have ever been to before. (Novel)

Hautman, Pete. **Slider.** New York, NY: Scholastic, Inc., 2017. 278p. $16.99. 9780763690700.

David learns the hard way that bidding online can have disastrous consequences, and now professional eating contests are his only way to pay his parents back before they get their credit card statement. (Novel)

Jolley, Dan. **The Emerald Tablet.** New York, NY: Harper, 2016. 294p. (Five Elements). $16.99. 9780062411655.

A seemingly innocent ritual of the elements is only supposed to cement their friendship but instead creates a crack between their world and a magical destructive one. Now, infused with elemental powers, they will have to find a way to put things right. (Novel)

Lê, Minh. **Drawn Together.** Illustrated by Dan Santat. New York, NY: Disney Hyperion, 2018. unpaged. $17.99. 9781484767603.

A grandfather and grandson do not speak the same language but discover they can communicate through their art. (Picture Book)

Lien, Henry. **Peasprout Chen: Future Legend of Skate and Sword.** New York, NY: Henry Holt and Company, 2018. 330p. (Peasprout Chen). $16.99. 9781250165695.

A student at a famous skate-and-sword school discovers who she can trust when someone starts vandalizing the school and they make sure she is a suspect. As the incidents escalate so does the potential for war between her home country and the country of her new school. (Novel)

Mass, Wendy, and Rebecca Stead. **Bob.** Illustrated by Nicholas Gannon. New York, NY: Feiwel and Friends, 2018. 201p. $16.99. 9781250166623.

After five years away, Livy returns to Australia to visit her grandmother and rediscovers Bob, a creature in a chicken suit. She does not remember him, but he remembers her and the promise she made to help him find his way home. (Novel)

McAnulty, Stacy. **The Miscalculations of Lightning Girl.** New York, NY: Random House, 2018. 293p. $16.99. 9781524767570.

Lucy was struck by lightning, and it left her a math genius who has trouble relating to her peers, which is even more complicated when you are starting middle school. (Novel)

Soundar, Chitra. **Mangoes, Mischief, and Tales of Friendship: Stories from India.** Illustrated by Uma Krishnaswamy. Somerville, MA: Candlewick Press, 2019. 179p. $16.99. 9781536200676.

A collection of short story fables set in India. Prince Veera and his best friend Suku fill in for the king and use creative methods to help solve the kingdom's problems. (Novel)

Stoddard, Lindsey. **Just Like Jackie.** New York, NY: Harper, 2018. 244p. $16.99. 9780062652911.

Robinson is her grandfather's right hand when it comes to working on cars in his automotive shop. Now her grandfather, who's also her guardian, is starting to forget things, and she's worried what will happen if anyone finds out. (Novel)

Family Programs for School Age Kids

With the emphasis on STEM, STEAM, and STREAM, libraries are offering more programs that tap into the subject areas of science, technology, reading, engineering, arts, and math. Kids are exposed to a variety of program options when they reach school age, and the programs are tailored to their age level and ability. Kids have the opportunity to try out computer programming and coding skills that could lead them to careers when they are older. Programs for school age kids are not just for after-school or evening attendees. There are also programs like Summer Reading or other book challenges that inspire learning through reading.

STEAM Expo—Cuyahoga County Public Library, Ohio, Parma Snow Branch

Becky Ranallo and Megan Barrett lead the information and technology learning department at Cuyahoga County Public Library, and their focus is innovative programming for young children all the way up to seniors. As libraries embraced the Common Core changes to education and the push for science, math, engineering, and technology skills in particular, the kids and parents have benefited. At libraries, kids can now build and test robots and create computer programs. While community organizations may offer similar content, they usually charge fees for their sessions but libraries do not.

Background

For Ranallo and Barrett, a light bulb went off when they were attending a local high school's Noise Expo, which brought together county and student entrepreneurs. They saw how impactful it was for students to get to interact with multiple organizations at one time. So, they began to think about how they could translate it to benefit the STEAM programs already happening at the library branch level. They decided to try a STEAM Expo. The goal was threefold: increase the number of adult STEAM volunteers, showcase and spread awareness of the variety of programs the library offers to caregivers, and give staff the opportunity to learn from each other.

Planning

An e-mail was sent out to library staff seeking volunteers to present. The only requirements were that it had to be something that could be demonstrated to a group of people and it had to have a hands-on component for people to try out. A cool outcome was that staff at all levels, and not just the MLS librarians, had an opportunity to shine. National Aeronautics and Space Administration (NASA) interns were also invited to come and they did wind-tunnel demonstrations. Cuyahoga County Public Library is lucky to have the NASA Glenn Research Center located within their service area.

A local company called Games Done Legit was hired through grant funds to do virtual-reality programming with an educational slant. For additional support, current STEAM volunteers were on hand to help with activities and speak to potential new volunteers about what is involved. The activities, listed in Table 6.1, were appropriate for all ages but would be appreciated on different levels depending on the age of the participants. For example, little kids would enjoy making something fizzy, while older kids and adults would understand more of the science behind a bath bomb.

Table 6.1   STEAM Expo

STEAM Expo—Activities/Demos	
Cuyahoga County Public Library	
CCPL Staff-Led Stations:	
Activity/Demo	*Staff Facilitator(s)*
Chem-Mystery Program	Teen Librarian and STEAM Volunteer
Raspberry Pi	Teen Librarian and STEAM Volunteer
Bath Bomb Science	Teen Librarian
Screen Printing	Adult Assistant
Whatever Floats Your Boat	Teen Librarian
Digital Photography/Seed Tape/ Math Literacy Games	Generalist Librarian
Ukulele @ CCPL	Children's Librarian & Teen Librarian
Tween Time Magnetic Art	Children's Assistant and Generalist Librarian
Coding with Light BOT	Teen Librarian
Innovation Centers	Information Technology Literacy Staff
Makey Makeys & Minecraft	Information Technology Literacy Staff
LEGO Robotics	Information Technology Literacy Staff
Volunteers @ CCPL	Volunteer Coordinator
Outside Organizations:	
Activity/Demo	*Organization*
Wind Tunnel Life Experiment	NASA
Virtual Reality Experience	Games Done Legit

Reprinted with permission from Megan Barrett and Rebecca Ranallo, Cuyahoga County Public Library.

Promotion

Advertising for the event involved some typical outlets like e-mails to library customers and posting to the library's social media platforms. The STEAM Expo was listed in the printed Branch Programming Guide that lists all library events, on the library's website both on the main landing page and in the events calendar. Library staff, especially those who were presenting, talked it up in their local communities, and the host branch encouraged people to check out the program that day. Help reaching an even larger audience was provided by the Encore Cleveland Foundation, a grant funder, who allowed the library to post to their blog and who then in turn reposted it to their social media platforms. This gave great, free, publicity through an already-established partnership.

The Program

The STEAM Expo was five hours long and there was no registration required to attend. Approximately 150 kids, teens, and adults came to experience at least some of the fun and educational activities. As families approached the various tables, caregivers were encouraged to participate in the activities too. Most were just as engaged as the kids, including one father with two teenage daughters. He jumped right in and made a bath bomb for his wife. It was a chance to talk informally about the programs themselves, and the STEAM parts were broken down for each activity. This showed parents that the library offers fun, but also educational programming for all ages.

Overall, parents were happy to learn that the library offered these programs. One 12-year-old boy wanted to know when they were going to do it all again. Having the extended time period of 10:00 A.M. to 3:00 P.M. allowed some families to come for a brief visit and for others to stay up to two hours. For families it was a similar experience to attending the local Children's Museum or Science Center as there were lots of things to explore, learn, and touch.

For Next Time

In the future, a theme might become part of the planning process. In order to make the event more of a destination, the demonstrations might be at specific times while the hands-on activities would be available throughout the whole event. A STEAM Expo Light is also in the works. It will be a smaller version that could be done right on the library floor rather than in a meeting room. The goal would be to capture the attention of more library visitors.

Making It Happen

Ranallo and Barrett spent about $1,300. Roughly $300 for supplies and staff tee shirts and $1,000 for the grant funded outside presenter. If your library budget is healthy or you can get grant support, this budget might be within reach for you. If not, an expo can also be done on a shoestring budget. You really only need tables and supplies for each station. Cutting out the expensive outside presenter and tee shirts could get your budget down to only a couple of hundred dollars. Perhaps a plea to the local Friends of the Library Group would be all you need to get the greenlight and budget needed.

The best part is that this program works for libraries pulling in staff from many branches, but it also works for libraries that are either a stand-alone or have a couple of branches. Size is not a factor. All that is needed is to take a look at the cool, perhaps unexpected for a library, programs you already offer. Then take a piece or part from them and you have your stations. In one afternoon, you can show caregivers and the community how you support your schools and the enrichment of a child's education that starts with reading and continues on to other areas of literacy like science and math. For school libraries you could create an expo for families that showcases the technology and makerspace equipment you use with students. School librarians may also want to partner with science teachers for the schools' science fair.

Families Coding Together—Cuyahoga County Public Library, Ohio, Warrensville Branch

You may not have the staffing, space, or time to host a large program like the STEAM Expo, but many libraries are already offering coding programs and camps for school age kids in their community. These programs are super popular in Cuyahoga County. The number of participants is usually limited because of the need of computers or tablets for the coding piece and also so that the instructor is able to give the kids the attention they need. For these programs, the parents are not required to attend. If they do, they might be sitting at the back or just coming in for the project presentation at the end. But it does not have to be this way. You can invite parents into the coding program so the whole family can learn together. The best part is that you may only need to tweak a type of programming you might already be presenting.

Background

Children's librarian Maria Trivisonno attended a conference on family learning, and one of the presentations was using the PBS Scratch Jr. program to teach kids and caregivers about coding. She thought the curriculum and app that had been created were well done and wanted to give it a try at her library. Since the program involved both the adults and kids, she asked JoAnna Schofield, the generalist librarian, who works with customers of all ages, to be her partner on the program. This ended up being a great chance for adult and youth staff to work together on a program.

The Program

The program is offered over four sessions that each last two hours. PBS recommends doing it over a four-week period but Schofield and Trivisonno offered it over a two-week period on Wednesday and Thursday evening each week. This worked better for their community. The first 30 minutes of each session was a family-style dinner. They ordered in pizza, which the library paid for. Schofield suggests talking to local restaurants about donating food for these meals. It never hurts to ask, if the cost of providing food would be a barrier to your library.

After dinner, the caregivers and kids were divided up into two groups. The adults went to a separate space with Schofield. She talked with caregivers about the importance of STEM activities and the need for caregivers to participate in these endeavors. It was also a great opportunity to impart some media mentorship tips to the caregivers. They discussed what makes a good app and what to be cautious of if the app is free. Then they moved on to a learning game. The adults were also taught the basics of the scratch activity for the week before rejoining the kids. The kids with Trivisonno played the same learning game that their caregivers were doing. They also learned the scratch lesson for that session. Then the families came back together to practice the new scratch skill together.

Basics Needed to Present the Program

The program is mapped out in the free PBS curriculum called "Family Creative Learning: Facilitator Guide." Each week you may need extra supplies for the activities, but the bare minimum you will need each week includes:

- Two staff members
- Two meeting spaces
- One projector and presenter computer
- Laptop or tablet for each child

If at all possible, they recommend that there is a 1:1 ratio between caregiver and child. This was accomplished at Warrensville because not only did parents attend but so did grandparents. This allowed the adults to divide and conquer if there were multiple kids in the family.

Of course, there are other work-arounds if you do not have the ideal 1:1 ratio. Perhaps older kids can work more independently and the caregiver can spend more time with the younger child who might need more help or vice versa if the older child wants to do something elaborate and the younger sibling is okay just playing and experimenting without a lot of adult help.

Keeping the program to around a dozen participants hits the sweet spot. Schofield said they had up to 18 people at one time, but the majority of the sessions were at 12. This was a good number of kids and adults to work with so everyone could get the time and attention they needed from the presenters.

Advertising the Program

Cuyahoga County Public Library uses an online events calendar to advertise programs and for customers to register. Schofield and Trivisonno used this as the main way to get the word out about the multiday program for families. Other avenues used included the white message board in the children's room and an e-mail blast to families who regularly attend programs. If you do an e-mail blast, it can boost your numbers. Just make sure you use the blind copy feature when putting in the e-mail addresses so you are not sharing customer e-mails without their permission. While the target age group is ages five to eight, older and younger siblings were welcome to join the family at this program.

Response from Parents

When offering a program, especially a new one and a series one at that, it is great to survey the participants to find out what they thought. Schofield and Trivisonno did this and got some great feedback. Caregivers reported being excited about the opportunity to work with their kids. Parents liked that both groups did the same activity when they were broken into separate groups. This allowed them to talk about what each experienced afterward. Parents said they would use the PBS Jr. Scratch App after the program was over.

Why You Should Try This Program

There were some great benefits to offering this series of programs on coding and inviting the adults to be participants rather than just be bystanders.

1. The confidence level of the adults grew each week as they learned more about coding and could then help their kids.

2. The skill level of the projects was impressive, and the families worked hard to reach their goals together.

3. The kids got a chance to practice their public-speaking skills in front of a friendly audience. At the end of the fourth session, the kids each presented their project, which was projected up on the screen so all could see (Schofield 2018).

50 Book Challenge—Euclid Public Library, Ohio

Keeping reading as a fun, pleasurable activity is harder as kids get older. With the start of elementary school, things like homework, extracurricular activities, and new friendships eat into the precious free-time minutes a child has. A creative way to show parents they need to keep reading on the list is to make it fun, and a challenge or competition is just one fun way to do it.

Background

You have probably heard of the 1,000 Books Before Kindergarten or the 1,000 Early Literacy Moments. Both are great ways for families to practice reading and other literacy skills before a child starts school. Then the focus shifts to learning to read during those early school years, but Christine Pyles, youth services manager, at Euclid Public Library wanted a way to engage families beyond grade two. She had two goals for the program: encourage kids in grades three to six to read more and to increase the number of children's materials checked out by families. The 50 Book Challenge was the perfect way to meet both of these objectives.

Planning

Pyles is lucky to have a great staff to pull from, including three full-time librarians, two full-time associates, and two part-time associates. As a group they began looking for titles that kids could choose from to complete the challenge. They wanted to have 100 titles initially and then planned to add more over time. Of course, they were looking for a variety of reading levels, different genres and subjects, and diverse titles. Important to remember is that the list is not a literary list but one that would have titles of high interest for kid readers. For each title that made the list, three questions to go with it were created by the title's recommender.

Staff were not assigned a specific number of titles or areas to read for. Instead, all were encouraged to help build the list, but reading was not done on work time. Pyles found it was helpful to look back at her Goodreads account for titles to suggest for the list. Once the initial 100 titles were settled upon, the list was given to the library's graphics department for creating a trifold brochure. It has a place for the child's name on the front cover and spots to check off titles as they are read. The back cover explains the challenge to parents and kids. Find an example of the original 50 Book Challenge brochure in Appendix F.

Promotion

The program went live in January 2018 after about six months of title list building, question writing, and brochure printing. To get the word out, they created posters, displays, and flyer handouts. They advertised on Facebook and Twitter.

Like many new programs, word of mouth was one of the best ways to get the message out. At the time of the launch, Pyles and her team were able to visit the local schools and talk about the 50 Book Challenge. In February, a special page was added to the library's website to promote the challenge to families browsing online.

January saw a big rush of people coming in to sign up, and then it slowed down a little. As of April 2018, there were about 50 kids participating, and the staff planned to promote again during spring school visits as well as to those signing up for the library's Summer Reading Game.

The Program

As you would expect, the program requires each child participating to read 50 books off the list provided by the library. Kids can read at their own pace, and there is no set date to have all 50 books read. The hope is that kids who start in third grade will complete the challenge by the end of sixth grade.

As a way to gauge what is being read and engage families, kids must come into the library after they finish a book. The library staff ask the children up to three questions about the book they have finished, and if they get at least one question right, then they get credit for the book. As kids sign up, they are entered into a spreadsheet created by the library, which is also used to track the titles each kid has read. While kids can keep track on the trifold brochure, the staff decided to also keep track in case the paper copy is lost.

Books from the list are pulled out and have their own section of shelving. This allows the 50 Book Challenge participants to browse specifically for titles on the list. The librarians and assistants do the pulling, not the shelving staff. They are considering adding stickers to the book spines so they would be easier to be identified by both the staff and families.

Incentives are given along the way to offer a little reward for the reading taking place.

- 10 books = color-changing pencil
- 25 books = Euclid Public Library slap bracelet
- 35 books = metal bookmark that says, "I've Read 35 Books for the 50 Book Challenge"
- 45 books = free copy of a book on the list for the reader to keep
- 50 books = Euclid Public Library tee shirt, reusable tote, a book light, headphones, and certificate of completion

While reading simply for the pleasure of reading is ideal, Pyles felt that small tokens to encourage continued participation would help motivate kids who might otherwise not participate.

A conscious decision was made to not have any pieces needed to participate available online. Registration, question answering, and prize picking up were all done in the library. Pyles felt it was important to get repeat visits out of the families as a way to get to know them better and to encourage the checking out of more library materials.

Ongoing Pieces

In order to keep the list of suggested titles fresh, it does involve some upkeep. This can be done once or twice a year or whatever time frame works best for your library. Replacing titles that are popular will also be necessary.

Book List. From the start Pyles knew that the number of titles kids could choose from would grow. Feedback from the first 100 titles led to them looking for more titles that would appeal to boys. They also looked for some high-interest but lower-reading level titles for kids at the younger end who weren't quite ready for the targeted grade-level titles. With these factors in mind, 80 new titles were added 6 months later.

In order to keep using the current supply of brochures, the new titles were created as an insert. After the initial supply runs out, they will revise the list and take off titles that are not popular with the readers and add new titles that have been published since the original list was created. The idea is to make the brochure a living document so it continues to appeal to new readers.

Collection Maintenance. To start the challenge, two to three replacement copies of each title were ordered from a book vendor. They decided to go with coated paperbacks from Baker and Taylor rather than library binding as it would allow them to stretch their budget a little farther. To pay for the project, they looked at what parts of the collection were and were not performing well. In the end, Pyles decided to decrease the audiovisual budget in order to increase the book budget.

Realizing that the replacement of titles is not going to be a one-time purchase is key. As new titles are added, you will need to add fresh replacement copies. As old favorites continue to stay on the list, they will start to show their wear and will also need to be replaced. This is a great problem, as it means your collection is circulating, but it also means you have to budget accordingly to support your program.

Outcome

Pyles was pleased to report that 85 percent of participants were doing the challenge with the help of a caregiver. Two of the parents were reading the books along with their kids and even listening to the books together in the car. One child was reading with his father. As of September 2018, 60 kids were signed up for the 50 Book Challenge. Four kids had read 20 books or more, 8 kids had read between 5 and 15 books, and 28 kids had read between 1 and 4 books. When the program launched in January, Pyles saw a 10 percent increase in circulation.

Making It Happen

If you are looking to engage kids in elementary and middle school, creating your own reading challenge may be the direction you want to go.

Public Library. You will need to start by creating a budget for the books you want extra copies of, program materials, and prizes you want to give away. Once you have the funding in place, look to generate your list of books and questions, replace copies of the books, and order the prizes you will need. Then create the program materials and start advertising.

School Library. Ask the principal and classroom teachers about having a schoolwide challenge. Decide which grades will participate, how many books kids will be expected to read, and what types of prizes they will receive. Other questions will involve funding for extra books and prizes. Perhaps a parent group will be able to help or you can look for community donations. Also, decide if kids will go to the school librarian to answer their book questions or if they will be able to do it with their classroom teacher.

A reading challenge will likely not replace your Summer Reading Program at either the public or school library. However, it can run alongside the Summer Reading Program and offer additional reading incentive during the school year.

Building Your Readers Advisory Toolbox

For the elementary- through middle-school crowd, you should strive to add to your repertoire:

- A minimum of three science-related books for kids per year
- A minimum of three math-related books for kids per year
- A minimum of three art-related books for kids per year
- A minimum of three technology-related books for kids per year
- A minimum of three other nonfiction books for kids per year
- At least one "just for fun" book each month. Like the kids, you need to read a book that you have been dying to read. And yes, it can be an adult book!

References

Books

Angleberger, Tom. **The Strange Case of the Origami Yoda.** New York, NY: Amulet Books, 2010. 141p. (Origami Yoda). $12.95. 9780810984257.

Barnett, Mac. **The Case of the Case of Mistaken Identity.** Illustrated by Adam Rex. New York, NY: Simon & Schuster Books for Young Readers, 2009. 179p. $14.99. 9781416978152.

Barnett, Mac, and Jory John. **The Terrible Two.** Illustrated by Kevin Cornell. New York, NY: Amulet Books, 2015. 217p. (The Terrible Two). $13.95. 9781419714917.

Fry, Michael. **Bully Bait.** New York, NY: Disney Hyperion Books, 2013. 214p. (The Odd Squad). $12.99. 9781423169246.

Gutman, Dan. **Willie & Me.** New York, NY: Harper, 2015. 157p. (A Baseball Card Adventure). $15.99. 9780061704048.

Kinney, Jeff. **Greg Heffley's Journal.** New York, NY: Amulet Books, 2007. 217p. (Diary of a Wimpy Kid). $13.95. 9780810993136.

Lowry, Lois. **Anastasia Krupnik.** Boston, MA: Houghton Mifflin Harcourt Company, 1979. 104p. (Anastasia Krupnik). $6.99pa. 9780544336681pa.

Myracle, Lauren. **Oopsy Daisy.** Illustrated by Christine Norrie. New York, NY: Amulet Books, 2012 (2009). 332p. (Flower Power). $16.95. 9781419700194.

Pilkey, Dav. **The Adventures of Captain Underpants.** New York, NY: Scholastic Inc., 1997. 121p. (Captain Underpants). 5.99pa. 9780590846288pa.

Interviews

Barrett, Megan, and Becky Ranallo. In interview with the author. November 7, 2017.
Pyles, Christine. In interview with the author. May 4, 2018.
Schofield, JoAnna. In interview with the author. August 2, 2018.

Websites

"Development Process." Common Core State Standards Initiative. Accessed September 18, 2018. http://www.corestandards.org/about-the-standards/development-process/.
"Family Creative Learning: Facilitator Guide." PBS Kids. Accessed August 2, 2018. http://iel.org/sites/default/files/PBS%20KIDS%20FCL%20Facilitator%20Guide.pdf.

CHAPTER SEVEN

Does the Library Offer Anything for My Family?

Libraries are welcoming spaces for families. Children's staff are devoted to the literacy process and fostering a love of reading. But even with the best of intentions, libraries may fall short of being the diverse and inclusive place they seek to be. Striving to improve on this is a goal all libraries should have.

When talking about "diversity" and "inclusion," it is important to remember that the two words are not interchangeable. Diversity is a group of people who are different from each other in some way. One individual person does not represent diversity alone. Inclusion happens when we invite and include different (diverse) groups of people to participate. Diversity is inherent, while inclusion is an intentional action.

Public Libraries Are for Everyone

The best place to start when looking to become more inclusive is to get to know your community. Look at who is coming to your programs. Observe who is using your library to check out materials, to study, to play. Check what groups are using your meeting room space. This will help you get a better idea of who is already using your library. However, it will not tell you who is not.

Families Not Using the Library

Some families that you might not be serving include the lesbian, gay, bisexual, transgender/transsexual, queer/questioning, intersex, and asexual communities. Families with foster children, with children who are developmentally delayed, or where language is a barrier may also feel like outsiders. Around the world libraries are not always free to use. Families who are new to the United States may not realize the vast, zero-cost, resources that can be found at the local public library.

Immigrants may be unsure of the welcome they will receive at a library or during a program. This can also be said of families with children who are developmentally delayed. Rather than expecting these families to find us and assimilate into the library setting we are comfortable with, libraries need to seek out these families and tweak our services so they are more inclusive.

Discovering New Potential Library Users

Trying to learn who is not using your space will give you a chance to reach out to a wider population. Look at the latest census data. See who is attending events in the community. Visit the schools and notice the diversity you see in the classrooms but not in your library. Then look for ways to create a more inclusive atmosphere in your library. This can happen through the programs you offer in the library and in the community. It can also happen through the materials you collect at your library.

The Inclusive School Library

There will always be diversity in your school whether it relates to race and ethnicity, identity, or economic status. The school library, therefore, has the opportunity to be an inclusive space that offers kids materials and services that represent who they are and welcomes them in, no matter what they look like or where they are from.

Making All Kids Active Library Users

Students will come into your library as part of class visit time, but you will have to pay attention to the kids who are on the outskirts of the group. Is there a reason that certain kids never check out materials unless they have to for a class assignment? Perhaps it is because they are not finding materials with people who look like them on the cover or between the pages of the book. It might also be that kids are afraid of losing a book because their home life is unstable.

The first is easier to correct as you can seek out books that represent all of the kids your school library serves. It can be harder to address the fear of losing a book or the inability to pay for a lost book. One thing you can suggest is that kids check out a book to keep at school. With teacher support, these books can be used for student choice reading during the day. If the book does not leave the school building, there will be less chance of it getting lost or being returned late.

Respecting Diversity

Keep in mind the diversity, or the lack of diversity, of your school when you are creating lessons for classes and choosing books to read to kids at the library. In the fall, not every family celebrates Halloween. A better choice would be to focus on nature-related activities like picking apples and pumpkins rather than dressing up, trick or treating, or carving pumpkins. You may not be able to control the school's decision, but you can make the school library an inclusive space for all students.

When choosing books to share, you should also make sure that you are reading books that offer diverse representation whether you see your school as being diverse or not. With the younger grades, it can be tempting to read lots of books that have animal characters instead of children. There are lots of great books out there like this and some even touch on diverse topics. However, kids need to see other kids who look like them and who go through similar situations in the stories shared with them. So make sure you include picture books with people of varying skin tones, and when choosing chapter books and fiction books, make sure your diverse choices are not all historical fiction. It makes kids feel included, rather than feeling different or ignored, if they see contemporary kids in stories.

Collection Development and Merchandising: Diversity

Whether you are in a school or public library, you should be asking yourself these questions when it comes to your collection. Are you purchasing high-quality diverse titles that offer mirrors for the diverse kids and families to discover? What about having titles that represent kids who are different from the majority population who visits your library? Seeing ourselves and seeing others in the books we read is important to kids building their own identity as well as a sense of empathy toward others. It may even make a difference as to when they become a reader.

Promoting Diverse Books

Librarians absolutely should be promoting diverse books in their community, but what is the best way to accomplish this? I recently had a conversation with a couple of fellow Cuyahoga County Public Library staff members: Wendy Bartlett, collection development and acquisitions manager, and Kate

Merlene, adult librarian. We were discussing how to best promote the diverse books in our collection and how to make them discoverable for customers. The exchange turned to whether or not diverse books should be treated like a genre. Should you have labels for African American books in the same way you would mystery books? The answer we came to is no. African American is not a genre and neither is Lesbian, Gay, Bisexual, Transgender, or Queer (LGBTQ). Groups of people should not be placed in the same categories as genres like science fiction or romance.

Instead, diverse books should be included within the genre lists. So, if you are creating a list of fantasy titles for your library or for a teacher, you would make sure to include titles that represent diverse people as a part of the list. By doing this, you are making a conscious decision to be inclusive with your book list. Now your kids and families have a much better chance of finding not only a book in a genre they like but also one with characters that look like or who are relatable to them. This goes beyond just book lists. Diverse titles should be an integral part to all displays and should be used in storytimes and other library programs. However, this is not to say that you cannot have a display of African American interest titles up in your library or create a book list of the Best Diverse Books of the year. Just be thoughtful when choosing the labels you place on the spine of a book or in your library's catalog.

Does Anyone Really Read Diverse Books?

Publishers have stated in the past that they do not publish as many authors and titles by diverse people because the market does not support it. The good news is that publishers are starting to recognize that if they do not publish diverse books, then people and libraries cannot purchase them. There is still a long way to go, but imprints like Salaam Reads from Simon & Schuster are a step in the right direction.

But it is not just publishers that are resistant to diverse works. Libraries, both school and public, have been known to say that they do not purchase certain diverse titles because they do not represent their community or because the books just sit on the shelf. This may be the case but it does not have to be, and it should not be. Librarians need to be reading diverse books or, at the very least, they should be seeking out reviews and best of lists from trusted sources like School Library Journal or Kirkus. Readers advisory is the first step to getting diverse books off the shelf and into the hands of kids and caregivers.

When talking with families about favorite authors and titles, you must be able to include diversity in your recommendations. You will find book lists throughout this book, and there are diverse books mixed in throughout those lists. This is because I read diverse books. Some of my favorite authors include Jacqueline Woodson, Rita Williams Garcia, Grace Lin, Jason Reynolds, Euka Holmes, and Hena Khan. I recommend and gush about these authors' books on a frequent basis, and I recommend these authors and their books to white kids too. Think about it, you would not hesitate to recommend a book with a white child to a child of color, would you?

Building Your Collection

As the sole selector in a large public library, I am looking at reviews every day to help me make purchasing decisions. While that is the focus of my job, it is not for the branch staff that I am sending the books to. The branch staff are dealing with programming, homework help, and feeding kids—among other duties. To help get quality books on staff radar, I write a weekly internal blog called Medal Worthy, which serves as a mock awards platform. I tackle the Newbery, Caldecott, and Printz but also the Coretta Scott King, Pura Belpre, and Stonewall Awards. My recommendations get the word out on new diverse titles in the collection. In turn, the youth staff in the branches are talking about and displaying diverse books and it is paying off. Here are just a smattering of diverse titles and a glimpse of how they were circulating at Cuyahoga County Public Library in September 2018.

Applegate, Katherine. **Crenshaw.** New York, NY: Feiwel and Friends, 2015. 245p. $16.99. 9781250043238.
> Own 28 copies—16 copies checked out.
> Jackson remembers living out of the family car. When the financial stability of his family is called into question again, his imaginary friend comes back to offer support. (Novel)

Arnold, Elana K. **A Boy Called Bat.** Illustrated by Charles Santoso. New York, NY: Walden Pond Press, 2017. 198p. (Bat). $16.99. 9780062445827.
> Own 13 copies—13 copies checked out.
> Bat is autistic and has trouble connecting with other people sometimes. However, he immediately attaches to the baby skunk his mother, a vet, has rescued. (Novel)

Blake, Ashley Herring. **Ivy Aberdeen's Letter to the World.** New York, NY: Little, Brown and Company, 2018. 310p. $16.99. 9780316515467.
> Own 3 copies—3 copies checked out—1 hold.
> Ivy's family loses everything in a tornado. As the family sorts out their finances, Ivy worries someone will discover her lost sketching notebook and realize she likes girls. (Novel)

Bunting, Eve. **Yard Sale.** Illustrated by Lauren Castillo. Somerville, MA: Candlewick Press, 2015. unpaged. $15.99. 9780763665425.
> Own 7 copies—4 copies checked out.

A family must sell their belongings in a yard sale and move to an apartment. Their young daughter does not really understand why, other than it is about money. But one thing this family learns is that their love will be with them wherever they live. (Picture Book)

Colato Laínez, René. **Mamá the Alien: Mamá la Extraterrestre.** Illustrated by Laura Lacá mara. New York, NY: Children's Book Press, 2016. unpaged. $17.95. 9780892392988.

Own 5 copies—1 copy checked out.

A child finds her mother's Resident Alien card and believes her mother is an alien from outer space. Told in English and Spanish, it shows the confusion a word can create and also the steps an immigrant has to go through to become a citizen of the United States. (Picture Book)

Davies, Nicola. **The Day War Came.** Illustrated by Rebecca Cobb. Somerville, MA: Candlewick Press, 2018. unpaged. $16.99. 9781536201734.

Own 4 copies—4 copies checked out.

A refugee's journey as seen through the eyes of a child. Inspired by the true story of a refugee child not allowed to attend school because the school did not have a chair for her. (Picture Book)

Dillon, Diane. **I Can Be Anything! Don't Tell Me I Can't.** New York, NY: The Blue Sky Press, 2018. unpaged. $17.99. 9781338166903.

Own 13 copies—9 copies checked out.

When that little negative voice inside a girl's head starts talking—squash it. Girls can do anything! (Picture Book)

Federle, Tim. **Better Nate Than Ever.** New York, NY: Simon & Schuster Books for Young Readers, 2013. 275p. (Nate). $16.99. 9781442446892.

Own 18 copies—3 copies checked out.

Nate wants to act in a Broadway show and runs away to New York to make it happen. In this first book, he is only starting to accept he is gay. (Novel)

Gino, Alex. **George.** New York: Scholastic Press, 2015. 195p. $16.99. 978054 5812542.

Own 8 copies—1 copy checked out.

George knows he is a girl, even if biology does not agree. Now she must find a way to tell her family and her best friend that she is transgender. (Novel)

Gray Smith, Monique. **My Heart Fills with Happiness.** Illustrated by Julie Flett. Victoria, BC: Orca Book Publishers, 2016. unpaged. $9.95. 9781459809574.

Own 27 copies—8 copies checked out—1 copy reference.

First Nation families celebrate what brings joy between the parents and the child. (Board Book)

Helget, Nicole. **End of the Wild.** New York, NY: Little Brown and Company, 2017. 266p. $16.99. 9780316245111.

Own 2 copies—2 copies checked out.

A family barely getting by could benefit from the new fracking company, but it comes at a high cost to the woods that bring food, peace, and joy to Fern. (Novel)

Hunt, Lynda Mullaly. **Fish in a Tree.** Nancy Paulsen Books, 2015. 276p. $16.99. 9780399162596.

    Own 13 copies—10 copies checked out.

    Ally has done an excellent job of covering up the fact that she has trouble reading until a new teacher discovers she is dyslexic. (Novel)

Leet, Rhonda. **Franny's Father Is a Feminist.** Illustrated by Megan Walker. Brooklyn, NY: Pow!, 2018. unpaged. $17.99. 9781576878736.

    Own 7 copies—4 copies checked out.

    Franny's father is a stay-at-home dad who supports his daughter's endeavors, including playing hockey and taking ballet lessons. (Picture Book)

Love, Jessica. **Julián Is a Mermaid.** Somerville, MA: Candlewick Press, 2018. unpaged. $16.99. 9780763690458.

    Own 3 copies—2 copies checked out.

    Julián is entranced by the women he sees dressed up as mermaids and creates his own costume. His beloved Abuela discovers him in his mermaid dress and supports his creativity. (Picture Book)

Medina, Juana. **Juana & Lucas.** Somerville, MA: Candlewick Press, 2016. 89p. (Juana & Lucas). $14.99. 9780763672089.

    Own 10 copies—4 copies checked out.

    Juana lives in Bogota, Colombia. She loves her dog, Lucas, but she does not love learning English at school. (Chapter Book)

Newman, Lesléa. **Sparkle Boy.** Illustrated by Maria Mola. New York, NY: Lee & Low Books Inc., 2017. unpaged. $17.95. 9781620142851.

    Own 5 copies—1 copy checked out.

    Challenging gender norms, Casey likes to play with trucks and wear sparkly skirts and nail polish. With the support of his family, Casey can express himself as he chooses. (Picture Book)

Peete, Holly Robinson, Ryan Elizabeth Peete, and Denene Millner. **My Brother Charlie.** Illustrated by Shane Evans. New York: NY: Scholastic Press, 2010. unpaged. $16.99. 9780545094665.

    Own 8 copies—2 copies checked out.

    Based on the author's family, Charlie is autistic and his twin sister, Callie, is not. Told from Callie's perspective, the story shows their differences but also the strong bond between the siblings. (Picture Book)

Perl, Erica S. **All Three Stooges.** New York, NY: Alfred A. Knopf, 2018. 233p. $16.99. 9780399551758.

    Own 8 copies—1 copy checked out.

    Noah is preparing for his bar mitzvah with his best friend Dash until Dash's father commits suicide. As the teen boys start to grow apart, Noah worries he may lose his best friend too. (Novel)

Polacco, Patricia. **Junkyard Wonders.** New York, NY: Philomel Books, 2010. unpaged. $17.99. 9780399250781.

    Own 15 copies—5 copies checked out.

    With the help of a caring teacher, a group of kids with learning differences are shown just how smart and talented they each are. (Picture Book)

Rosenthal, Amy Krouse, and Paris Rosenthal. **Dear Girl.** Illustrated by Holly
    Hatam. New York, NY: Harper, 2017. unpaged. $17.99. 9780062422507.
    Own 37 copies—13 copies checked out.
    Written as notes to girls that encourage them to be themselves and trust
    their own instincts. (Picture Book)
Saeed, Aisha. **Amal Unbound.** New York, NY: Nancy Paulsen Books, 2018.
    226p. $17.99. 9780399544682.
    Own 13 copies—11 copies checked out.
    A contemporary novel set in Pakistan that follows the life of a 12-year-old
    girl who, after insulting a powerful man, must leave home and become a
    servant for his family. (Novel)
Tarpley, Natasha Anastasia. **I Love My Haircut!** Illustrated by E. B. Lewis. New
    York, NY: Little, Brown and Company, 2017 (2002). unpaged. $6.99.
    9780316276061.
    Own 9 copies—1 checked out.
    A young African American boy goes to the barbershop with his father. It's
    time for his very first haircut. (Board Book)
Yang, Kelly. **Front Desk.** New York, NY: Arthur A. Levine Books, 2018. 286p.
    $16.99. 9781338157796.
    Own 13 copies—8 copies checked out.
    Mia and her family are immigrants from China living in the United
    States. They experience the challenges of living among people who speak
    a language they are only just learning and have customs they are unaware
    of. (Novel)

Community-Focused Programming

The next time you sit down to plan out your programming for the month,
the quarter, or the year, take a moment to do a diversity audit. Look at your
program plans and notice if you are including diverse books and whether
you are offering programs at times that working families can attend. Then
take it a step further and look for ways to include additional programs and
services that would reach new families in your service area.

Barbershop Deposit Collections—Cuyahoga County Public Library, Ohio, Maple Heights Branch

I first heard through a post on Facebook about barbers encouraging African American kids to read to them while getting a haircut. I thought it
sounded like a great idea and was excited to learn that my library system had
been approached to help partner with a local organization to beef up the
selection of books the kids could choose from at the barbershops.

Background

Since I was not directly involved in creating the partnership, I sat down with Bonnie Demarchi, a youth branch services supervisor III, to learn more about how the program works at Cuyahoga County Public Library. From Demarchi, I learned that the executive director of the Barbershop Literacy Project, a retired educator, had made encouraging African American males to read her mission.

The director was already working with approximately 20 barbershops in Cleveland and the surrounding outer-ring suburbs when she approached the public library. Up to that point she had been bringing the barbers onboard, negotiating space for small bookcases, and purchasing the books from her own funds. Hoping to provide a wider selection of books for the boys to choose from, she wanted to see if the library would loan out books. A meeting was scheduled with the Barbershop Literacy Project, Cuyahoga County Public Library's collection development staff, and the branch managers from three locations that had barbershops that were part of her program already. They sat down to discuss logistics.

What's Involved

In order for the partnership to work, there had to be coordination among several departments at the library, including floor staff, circulation staff, collection development staff, and the shipping staff. For a smaller library system, there may be some overlap in these roles, but you need to make sure everyone is looped into the conversation so you do not have any last-minute road blocks.

Breaking it down, floor staff pull together the titles for the deposit collection—around 30–50 per quarter for each location. Mostly this means shopping the branch collection, but the staff can also call in titles from surrounding branches. The collection development team supports the program by ordering extra copies of popular titles like Newbery, Caldecott, and Coretta Scott King Honoree, *Crown: An Ode to the Fresh Cut* by Derrick Barnes and illustrated by Gordon C. James so the barbershops would have them on hand.

The circulation staff checks out the titles for the quarter so there is no need to worry about renewing or holds during the three-month period the books are at the barbershops. They also check back in the titles once they have been returned. Staff have found it really helpful to have two cards for each barbershop. One card has the titles that are currently on loan, and the second has the new collection on it. This helps keep straight what should be returned versus what has just been added to the barbershop bookcases.

After the circulation staff check out the books, they are put into bins and sent to the Cuyahoga County Public Library's shipping department. The drivers then deliver the books to the barbershops, but they do not unpack. They also pick up the previous quarter's materials, but they do not pack them up. Instead, a day or two before the delivery from shipping, the branch manager or a designee goes in and packs up the current materials at the barbershop. Then they go back within a day or two of the new shipment being delivered to unpack it. There are always some books on the shelves as the Barbershop Literacy Project has made permanent donations of titles. These titles tend to be classics.

Materials to Include in a Deposit Collection

The number of books sent is determined by the space at each location. As the barbers do not want the kids taking the books home, that also informs the length of books included. Demarchi says she mostly pulls picture books, beginning readers, high-interest nonfiction, and graphic novels. An occasional chapter book or teen book may be included, but the idea is for the books to be easy to browse and hopefully can be read in one visit.

These books are changed out quarterly, and at the Maple Heights Branch, Demarchi does the gathering. She is looking for African American titles with male characters. Contemporary is more popular, but she will also include some historical or history books. The rest of the titles are usually recent titles with high interest. Demarchi also includes some adult titles like cookbooks and books to help with resume creation for the use of student barbers. Most of the boys the barbers see are younger school age kids to middle graders, but kids of all ages are encouraged to read. The hope is to keep African American boys reading past the age where they typically stop.

Parent and Barber Buy In

One thing the library staff hears time and time again is that the kids love the books. They get excited when the new titles arrive. It is obvious when viewing the bookcases that the kids are rummaging through the shelves on a regular basis and selecting books they want to read. The barbers report enjoying talking about the books with kids during a haircut. Some are more comfortable than others, but most are giving it a try. "It is African American males (barbers) mentoring the younger generation" (Demarchi 2018). All are encouraging the kids to browse the shelves for books of interest, and this demonstrates to the caregivers that practicing reading skills is important.

Reality Check

Floor staff discovered early on that the barbers were not going to unpack the books delivered by the library's shipping department. As mentioned, floor staff had to step up and visit the locations. It usually takes about one and a half hours to visit all five locations served by the Maple Heights Branch. A nice side benefit is that it gives staff a chance to check in with the barbers and see how the section looks. It always feels good to see it looking browsed, aka well loved!

The model is also going to have to shift a little because the Maple Heights Branch is looking into adding some beauty salons near the library. They want to encourage the African American girls to read too.

Drag Story Hour—Anchorage Public Library, Alaska, Z. J. Loussac Library

Over the last few years, more and more libraries have started offering drag queen story hour in addition to their regular weekly storytimes. The inclusive nature of having drag queens and kings present storytime is a wonderful way to embrace community members who might not feel as welcome. It also provides the opportunity for families that want to show their children the diverse world we live in, the chance to do so.

Background

I first learned about Anchorage Public Library's Drag Story Hour from a post Elizabeth Moreau Nicolai, youth services coordinator, shared on the Association for Library Service to Children's electronic list in June 2018. Here she talked about dealing with backlash from someone in the community. She has a wealth of information about planning a Drag Story Hour and how to prepare for negative behavior before, during, and after the program. She does not use "Queen" in her program title as they also have a Drag King.

The Planning

It took roughly a year from Moreau Nicolai deciding she wanted to host a Drag Story Hour to the first one being offered. Part of this was being persistent and chasing leads on Drag Queens who might be interested in presenting. She first found some leads on Facebook, but there tended to be a lack of follow-through by those she contacted. Then she was connected to Identity Inc., a group of local advocates who helped her find volunteers.

The next step was to train the volunteers on how to present a storytime. The volunteers tended to have experience performing, usually in a bar setting, but not for a child audience. They were not familiar with reading stories, performing rhymes, or singing kid songs. The Anchorage staff did a brief overview on the pieces included in a storytime. They shared a storytime outline sheet that the Drag Queens and King could use for planning. The Jbrary website was also shared as a good resource for learning the motions to rhymes and songs.

The library staff did pull books for the Drag presenters to choose from. Some might be LGBT themed, but others focused more on creativity, which is a very broad topic and allows for lots of books from any library's collection to be considered perfect choices.

When to Offer

Moreau Nicolai did not just want to offer one Drag Story Hour during June for Pride Month as she felt strongly that it should be an "affirmation that inclusion is important to the community" (Moreau Nicolai 2018). So it was decided to host the first one in May 2018 and then a second one would be offered in June. After the success of both of these programs, in the future Drag Story Hour will be offered three times a year in February, June, and October.

Advertising

Anchorage did not do a lot of extra promotion for the Drag Story Hour. They wanted to stay a little under the radar and see what the community response would be. They did create an event on the library's Facebook page and on the library's online event calendar. In June, they also included it in an e-mail newsletter. They found that on social media they got more positive comments than negative from all over the world. People from England and Georgia were giving shout-outs of encouragement.

Attendance

For the first two Drag Story Hours, the program was offered in the regular storytime space on Saturdays. This room holds 75 people and they reached capacity both times. In May, they had to turn away about 20 people. In June it was closer to 30. From her personal relationships with some of the attendees, Moreau Nicolai knew there were LGBTQ families in attendance. It was also exciting to find families who were visiting the library for the first time, solely for the purpose of attending the Drag Story Hour.

Target Audience

The program was advertised for families with children aged five and under. So it was not surprising to see families with young children and elementary school age children attend. A little more unexpected were the adults without children and the teens. Moreau Nicolai felt the teens wanted to come because they were curious about Drag but were too young to go to a Drag performance since they typically take place in bars.

Going forward, Moreau Nicolai will move Drag Story Hour into the main theater that has room for 220 people, and there is better technology accessible to project stories, song lyrics, and rhymes so all can follow along with the presenters. In large groups simply sharing a picture book in its normal size will make it hard for many participants to view it.

Community Reaction

Moreau Nicolai worked with two organizations—Urban Libraries and Drag Queen Story Hour—to prepare for any community questions and potential negativity. There was little negativity from outside sources before the May program other than a grandmother who was upset when she thought the library was charging for the program. Anchorage uses a ticket system for their programs, but there is no cost. Once explained, the grandmother was happy that money would not be a barrier to bringing a child.

In June, the lead-up was also pretty smooth, but during the actual program, a man who is a preacher interrupted the program to express his religious opinions on Drag and LGBTQ. The Drag Queen and King handled things beautifully by starting to sing and getting the families to sing along and drown out the man as he was escorted out. This quick thinking kept the kids calm and allowed for the program to continue on.

The library looked to their current policies and procedures to explain to the man why he was removed from the room. These included:

- It was a ticketed event and the man did not have a ticket.
- The room was at capacity and his presence put the room over fire capacity.
- Customers are not allowed to harass other customers, staff, or presenters.

While the man did continue to protest his treatment, the library made it clear that these were the factors for his removal and not what he had to say. Being prepared ahead of time allowed the library to control the conversation.

Implementing at Your Library

If you are thinking about hosting your first Drag Queen Story Hour but want to see one first, you can find a list of upcoming programs on the Drag Queen Story Hour website. This is a great way to become familiar with the program. This will likely boost your desire to offer such a program in your own library.

Depending on the size and structure of your library and whether you are a public or school library, you will probably want to have a conversation with your administration before you move forward. You want to make sure they are on board and support the offering of a Drag Queen Story Hour. Perhaps show pictures or clips from the storytime you attend, if they allow you to record the program. Be ready to convince if there is some hesitation. Once you have administrative support, you can move on to the next step.

Now you will want to talk with families you see regularly at the library and who attend other programs you offer. Ask them about their interest in a Drag Queen Story Hour. Mention how the program's goal is to spark creativity and creative expression. Hopefully, you will hear from parents that they would be interested or that they would like more information about the program.

Again, if you are hearing resistance, listen to the concerns and see if you can alleviate them. If there is more resistance than you expected, do not get discouraged. Families that would like a diverse program may not be currently using your library. Be prepared for the negative but keep going!

Once you feel that you are ready for any potential challenges from naysayers, it is time to start looking for partners. You will want to look for organizations and contacts in your community who can help you find Drag Queens and Kings to work with. This may take a little time, like it did for Moreau Nicolai, but it will be worth it in the end.

As the youth services coordinator, Moreau Nicolai believes you should avoid surprising people by the content of a program. What she means is that you do not want to offer a Drag Story Hour one week as part of your regular Preschool Storytime. This may come as a surprise for parents who will not have had time to prepare themselves or their children. She feels that caregivers deserve the right to make a conscious decision to attend or not. Moreau Nicolai treats holiday programs like Halloween and Christmas in the same way. If they offer these programs, they are on a special date and time. She feels this helps build trust between the parents and the library staff.

A final thought to help you decide if you are ready for Drag Queen Story Hour is that after two programs, 150 people enjoyed the program and asked for more. One lone man and his camera accomplice were the only people to come in to the library to protest. The numbers do not lie here. A Drag Story Hour can be a way to connect with your community in an inclusive way.

National African American Read-In—Cuyahoga County Public Library, Ohio, Warrensville Heights Branch

The first National African American Read-In was hosted in 1990. It is sponsored by the Black Caucus of the National Council of Teachers of English. A Read-In is meant to be a way to celebrate Black History Month, and they take place on the first Sunday or Monday of February. This program works very similar to the Día program the Association of Library Service to Children offers each April. It includes a toolkit and the ability to register your program on a national registry. While the National African American Read-In started in the education community, hosting a Read-In aligns perfectly with the sentiment that libraries are the hub of a community.

Background

Maria Trivisonno is a children's librarian II for Cuyahoga County Public Library's Warrensville Branch. She is a white woman working in a predominately black community. Several years ago, Trivisonno wanted to do something special to honor African American History Month with her kids.

Her hope was to promote literacy with a program that needed little preparation and would not cost much to execute, as she did not have a large programming budget. The first two years she tried a book club. Year one with *Show Way* by Jacqueline Woodson, illustrated by Hudson Talbott, saw nine kids attend, but in year two with *Ron's Big Mission* by Rose Blue and Corinne J. Naden, illustrated by Don Tate, no one attended.

Rather than get discouraged, Trivisonno went back to the drawing board to figure out what would be the best way to engage her kids and promote literacy. It was at this point that she heard about the National African American Read-In that a librarian friend was doing at a neighboring library system. After checking out the NCTE website, she began planning for a Read-In of her own in February 2017. She was excited because not only would the program promote literacy but it also was an opportunity to offer an intergenerational program.

The Program

Trivisonno followed this format when creating her one-hour African American Read-In. About 40 minutes were allotted for the reading portion. Kids have a chance to look at the reading selections so they can pick one they feel comfortable reading aloud. Everyone does not have to read aloud. The librarian kicks things off with a short piece, usually from a longer novel. Then the kids and adults read the pieces they have selected. She also likes to break it up a little with some music. The last 20 minutes is snack time.

The host of the program will need to have reading selections prepared ahead of time. While some participants may come with their own pieces including their own original creations, it is more likely that kids, in particular, will need a simple selection to read from. Trivisonno recommends using picture books and poetry by African American authors like Ashley Bryan, Jacqueline Woodson, and Leo and Diane Dillon. The book *Let's Clap, Jump,*

Sing & Shout; Dance, Spin & Turn It Out!: Games, Songs, and Stories from an African American Childhood by Patricia C. McKissack, illustrated by Brian Pinkney, has some great rhymes for the littlest kids.

Depending on your situation, you might need to place an age restriction on participants. Trivisonno said her target was all ages but found she mostly had kindergarten through eighth grade and adults. You can be pretty broad about the ages attending as long as you make sure everyone understands that the reading selections need to be appropriate for the variety of ages in attendance.

Advertising

The Warrensville Branch is a suburb of the city of Cleveland. Many students visit the library after school until a parent or guardian is home. This after-school crowd offers a built-in audience for the program but is unlikely to bring in caregivers. To have an adult presence, Trivisonno reaches out to other members of the community.

She enters the information in the library's events calendar and printed program guide. One additional step she takes is to send invites to community members. People you might consider including are teachers, school board members, city council members, and the mayor. She also looks at the adult groups using the meeting rooms and invites the Adult Book Club and the Poetry Group.

Including Adults

For many libraries that host an African American Read-In in their school or public library, it might be possible to have the parents attend with their children. Of course, this would be the ideal scenario as kids could read with their parents, read in front of their parents, or listen to their parents read. In any of these three scenarios, kids see that reading is important to the adults in their lives.

The ideal is not always practical or achievable. At Trivisonno's branch the odds of having parents or grandparents attend programs with school age kids is pretty low. Many are working multiple jobs and it simply is not feasible. For Trivisonno, the African American Read-In is an opportunity for kids to see African American adults as reading role models. As she likes to tell kids, "You read for school. People read for life" (Trivisonno 2018).

One caveat: the adults are reading aloud in front of the group, and a library staff member is always present in the room. The adults are not reading one-on-one or with small groups of kids. Libraries should always use caution when bringing in adults to children's programs. If kids will be left alone with the adults or work more directly with them in a group setting,

I would highly recommend you have a policy in place to do background checks first. This protects the library and the kids we serve.

Incorporating at Your School Library

I'm always a fan of a program that does not cost much and this is that type of program. The only expense would be if you serve refreshments, which are nice to have but not crucial to the success of the program. This program was created by educators and belongs in schools. School librarians can have classes read aloud from African American writers during library time in February, can partner with a teacher or grade and pick a day to host a Read-In, or can get the principal on board and do a school-wide assembly where kids volunteer to read aloud pieces.

Outcomes

Like most librarians, Trivisonno included a book display of titles to read from but also longer works by authors like Christopher Paul Curtis, Kwame Alexander, Jason Reynolds, and Rachel Renée Russell. Upon seeing the Dork Diaries series by Russell, the kids were surprised and delighted to learn the author was African American.

About 20 people participated in 2017 and again in 2018. The first year it was mostly adults reading, but in 2018 the middle-school crowd also wanted to read. Trivisonno made contact with one of the sixth-grade teachers who offered extra credit to kids who participated. In the future, she hopes to continue this relationship and to bring on board a few more teachers to help increase the number of participants.

World Language Storytime—Cuyahoga County Public Library, Ohio, Beachwood Branch

During the spring of 2018, I spent a couple of months working at the Beachwood Branch filling in as the children's librarian, and I was able to see firsthand how the staff is working to meet the needs of their community. Two programs that really spoke to me were the Hebrew Storytime and the Chinese Storytime. Both programs are collaborations with members of the community.

Background

Hebrew Storytime has been around the longest. Children's librarian Amy Dreger was aware that one of the populations her branch served was Jewish. Dreger witnessed these families using the library and thought it would be great to offer a storytime in Hebrew, but she didn't speak the language and there was not anyone on staff who knew enough Hebrew to feel comfortable presenting. By happenstance, a woman who worked for the Jewish Education Center called with a question and Dreger happened to be the other person on the phone. They got to talking, and Dreger learned that the Jewish Education Center was offering Hebrew Storytimes at the local Barnes and Noble. Dreger set up a meeting to discuss offering a program at the library, and both parties decided to give it a try. In 2018, roughly five years later, the program is going strong and only offered at the public library.

Chinese Storytime happened in a slightly different way. Again, Dreger knew that her community would be interested in a storytime in Chinese, but there was not a person on staff who could lead. Then Aimee Lurie, branch manager, started noticing that a Chinese group was routinely booking the meeting room to offer a Chinese program for families. Lurie and Dreger worked with the leaders to create a collaboration between the group and the library. Like the Hebrew Storytime, this group was also presenting at several locations, but once they found a permanent home at the library, they focused their program there.

What Is Involved

Cuyahoga County Public Library requires a staff member to be present at all children's programs even if the program is done by an outside presenter. So this is a factor when considering a reoccurring program like a world language storytime. However, both Dreger and Lurie feel that the benefits far outweigh the staff time involved. For both storytimes, the groups they partner with do the planning and presenting, with minimal help from library staff. The occasional craft supply or use of the shaky eggs are usually all that is required.

Both programs consist of a story or two, songs, and a craft. The presenters for Hebrew Storytime work at the local Jewish day school, so they are familiar with working with groups of children. The Chinese Storytime presenters are two enthusiastic parents who did not have this same experience. So, for Chinese Storytime, Dreger provided some basic training on things like early literacy skills, using manipulatives, as well as the importance of songs and rhymes.

Focus of the Storytimes

While both programs provide a storytime in another language, the way they are presented is slightly different. For Hebrew Storytime, the presenter is teaching words and phrases to kids and adults who want to learn the language but don't speak it as a first or second language. The storytime is a mix of Hebrew and English.

For Chinese Storytime, the presenters are doing the majority of the storytime in Chinese and the families attending speak Chinese. The parents and grandparents want to keep the language alive in the next generation. This is starting to change a little as families who have adopted Chinese children and other non-Chinese families are starting to attend as a way for their children to learn about another language and culture.

Dreger works with the presenters to make sure the program remains inclusive while not losing their initial purpose of providing storytimes that are in a child's or family's own language. To keep the lines of communication open, Dreger recommends having periodic meetings with the presenters to check and see how things are going. It gives her the opportunity to make suggestions on how things might work better for the library and to hear how the library could better support the program.

Attendance

Hebrew Storytime is offered once a month on Wednesdays at 4:00 P.M. and Chinese Storytime is offered twice a month on Saturdays at 10:30 A.M. Hebrew Storytime goes for about half an hour, and the ages of the children skew anywhere from babies to third graders. Mothers, nannies, grandparents, and fathers attend with the kids. Most months there are anywhere from 20 to 25 people in attendance. Chinese Storytime goes for closer to an hour and a half and the children tend to be babies through first grade. For many of the families it is a multigenerational event. Mother and father, grandmother and grandfather will all attend with the children. This program typically sees 40 to 50 people in attendance.

Advertising

The library includes the Chinese and Hebrew Storytimes in their printed program guide and their online events calendar. This reaches regular library users and perhaps a few families that stumble upon it while browsing the print or online program descriptions. However, this does not necessarily reach families that are not already using the library.

That is why collaboration is so terrific. The program leaders will promote the storytimes to their own contacts, which really helps get the word out to nonlibrary users. Lurie and Dreger have both noticed that families they have not seen in the library before will attend these world-language storytimes. Lurie also makes it a point to let families that are visiting the library know about the storytimes. For example, if she overhears someone speaking Hebrew, she will mention the program and invite them to attend.

All families are encouraged to attend traditional storytime and other programs and events the library offers and some do. However, they have found that these two storytimes tend to invite a different audience. This, of course, supports their decision to devote staff, resources, and meeting rooms to these reoccurring programs.

Making It Work in Your Library

Lurie suggests that you look at who is using your meeting rooms and library to gauge which languages to offer. Then see if someone you know might be willing to work with the library or have contacts they can share. Decide upfront what the library's role and the presenter's role will be so that there are fewer surprises along the way.

You will also need to figure out who will supply the books in the world language. For Hebrew Storytime the presenters bring titles from the school library, although the public library is planning to add Hebrew-language books to the collection starting in 2019. The public library started collecting Chinese picture books to support the storytime in 2017. These titles are purchased from China Sprout, as the presenters are looking for popular stories published in the United States that have been translated into Chinese.

As the person who selects the materials, I made the initial contact with China Sprout. I quickly learned that the dialect, like Mandarin, applies to how the language is spoken rather than written. Instead, when purchasing I needed to know if the books should be in traditional or simplified characters. After conferring with the presenters, we learned that simplified characters were what they would need.

My Personal Testimony

From my own experience, I can say that you will likely get families you have never seen before and they may skew older than you expect. I found this when I did a series of language storytimes during my traditional family storytime back in 2010. For Spanish it was mostly the typical crowd. For Arabic there were a few new families, and when we did French, there were school-age kids and their mother who spoke fluent French. She came to our library specifically because she had heard about the program. She was delighted to speak in French with the presenter at the end of the program.

I also had the opportunity to sit in on the Chinese Storytime several times. It was a powerful experience to be in a room where I was the only white person and to hear a language spoken around me that I did not understand at all. It gave me an even greater appreciation for what families new to a country must feel. I concur with Dreger and Lurie that overall, it is pretty easy to implement once you find your partner, and you will find it a rewarding way to connect with your community.

Adapted Storytime—Cuyahoga County Public Library, Ohio, North Royalton Branch

For families that have children with developmental differences, traditional storytime tends to be a barrier. While most caregivers say the issue is not the library staff, they do tend to feel unwelcome by the other parents. Their child's need to move around or sensitivity to the noise of a traditional program can cause them to be singled out by the rest of the families. Many libraries are recognizing this divide and are working to make sure children at all developmental levels can enjoy the storytime experience.

Background

In 2015, Cuyahoga County Public Library was offering training to staff on becoming an Adapted Storytime presenter. For Angie, this sounded like an opportunity that she wanted to learn more about. She went to the initial training with the understanding that she was not required to pursue the full training unless she wanted to. It was important that those becoming presenters had a desire to present programs to meet the needs of developmentally different families.

After attending the initial meeting, Angie was ready to move forward with the next steps. This involved observing others presenting the Adapted Storytime. Then as she became more comfortable, she copresented. After that she was ready to start presenting on her own.

The Program

The North Royalton Branch offers Adapted Storytime in the branch once a quarter, and once a month, they offer outreach to the Peer Model Preschool, which is part of the public schools. The preschool has seven classes that range in developmental ability. In the beginning, Angie was doing all of the presentations, as she was the only one trained. About a year into going to the preschool, Maria was also trained and so they could split the classes up. It also allowed them to co-present the Adapted Storytime at the branch.

Planning

An Adapted Storytime will have many of the same elements as your other storytimes, like songs, rhymes, fingerplays, and stories. Find a sample program outline in Appendix G. You'll probably use a similar welcome speech that includes asking caregivers to participate and letting them know it is okay to step out if a child becomes out of sorts. They are always welcome to exit and reenter as needed.

However, there are some differences too. Angie and Maria say to keep in mind these things when you put together your adapted program:

- Carpet squares allow kids to know where their personal space is.
- A basket of manipulatives or fidgets that is passed out at the start of the program provides kids with a way to help them focus.
- Keeping the lights dimmed if possible and the music softer offers a more calming environment.
- Go into the storytime room first and let the families come to you rather than ringing a bell to gather everyone together.
- Copresent so you can use double visuals. This can be one person reading the book, while the other tells the story with flannel or popsicle stick pieces.
- Avoid wearing bright colors, busy patterns, or strong fragrances.

Promotion and Partnership

Adapted Storytime is included in the Cuyahoga County Public Library program guide that lists all branch programs. It is also part of the online events calendar. Since the program is only offered once a quarter, the branches offering Adapted Storytime try to offer it on different days so families can attend more than one branch and, therefore, more storytimes each quarter.

Recently, the library partnered with Connecting for Kids, a resource for parents with kids who need adapted programs and outings. Angie and Maria have found that this partnership has helped increase the number of families attending the Adapted Storytimes each quarter from four families to seven families. They limit the number of children to 12, and siblings are encouraged to attend with the family. Families are encouraged to register, and reminder phone calls are made. During these calls, it is a chance for library staff to ask if there is anything they should know that would make the experience a better one for the child.

Outreach is an important way to reach more of the community. By partnering with the Peer Model Preschool, the library is able to connect with kids who might not be coming into the branch. Angie and Maria have found that families from the preschool have started coming into the library and are attending the Adapted Storytimes. In order to make the outreach visits successful, the library sends a letter at the beginning of each school year. It tells the preschool staff what they can expect during a visit and what is expected of the teachers and aides. The letter states, "We also ask for full participation in the storytime from teachers and aides, as this encourages and supports the children in their own participation" (Angie and Maria 2018). An explanation of what Adapted Storytime means at Cuyahoga County

Public Library and a link to the event calendar for additional programming information is also shared.

Parent Participation

Just like all the storytimes that the library offers, Adapted Storytime requires parent involvement and Angie has found that there tends to be an even greater response then in traditional storytime. The parents will help their child put flannel pieces on the flannel board or walk the balance beam. Modeling of behaviors takes place and there is repetition of activities, but to help kids know what is coming next, Angie and Maria use a schedule board.

Another important piece for the caregivers is the social play that takes place after Adapted Storytime. Toys are brought out and families can make connections while the kids play. This adds to the overall feeling of being welcome at the library.

The Response from Parents

Most parents say that it is nice to not be attracting extra attention while in storytime. "Having an Adapted Storytime allows them to attend without feeling judged by other parents," said one father. Very important to the parents is that the whole family can attend together. The program is not just for the sibling that needs the adaptations. The storytime I attended had one preschool boy who benefited from an adapted program, and his younger and older brothers also enjoyed attending with him.

Trying It at Your Library

You may be reading this and thinking, "I would love to offer this programming in my community." You may know that you have a real need from the families you see or do not see. You may feel all this but be stumped on where to even start. Do not feel bad! Being willing to learn and try is half the battle. The first thing you can do is look to the libraries near you. Do any of them offer an Adapted Storytime? If so, contact them and ask if you can come observe. Most librarians are more than happy to share and will welcome your interest. These programs may also be listed as Sensory or Special Needs Storytimes.

Depending on where you are located, that might not be possible, so another resource would be the special education teachers at your local public schools. Contact the schools for a name and see if you can come in to observe part of the day. See if they might be willing to help you plan an Adapted

Storytime and even copresent a few until you feel comfortable. Just like librarians, teachers like to share their knowledge.

Building Your Readers Advisory Toolbox

The world around us is full of people of all different races, religions, economic status, and beliefs. What we read and share must now go beyond the standard white boy or girl. Diverse families deserve to see themselves in the books shared by library staff. Read books from these broad categories to expand your knowledge.

- Twelve diverse picture books per year
- Six diverse first readers books per year
- Four diverse chapter books per year
- Three diverse nonfiction books per year
- Four books that kids with sensory differences would enjoy

References

Books

Barnes, Derrick. **Crown: An Ode to the Fresh Cut.** Illustrated by Gordon C. James. Chicago, IL: Bolden Books, 2017. unpaged. $17.95. 9781572842243.
Blue, Rose, and Corinne J. Naden. **Ron's Big Mission.** Illustrated by Don Tate. New York, NY: Dutton Children's Books, 2009. unpaged. $16.99. 9780535478492.
McKissack, Patricia C. **Let's Clap, Jump, Sing & Shout; Dance, Spin & Turn It Out!: Games, Songs, & Stories from an African American Childhood.** Illustrated by Brian Pinkney. New York, NY: Schwartz & Wade Books, 2017. 173p. $24.99. 9780375870880.
Russell, Rachel Renée. **Tales from a NOT-SO-Fabulous Life.** New York, NY: Aladdin, 2009. 282p. $13.99. 9781416980063.
Woodson, Jacqueline. **Show Way.** Illustrated by Hudson Talbott. New York, NY: G.P. Putnam's Sons, 2005. unpaged. $16.99. 9780399237492.

Interviews

Angie and Maria. In interview with the author. June 28, 2018.
Bartlett, Wendy, and Kate Merlene. In interview with the author. September 19, 2018.
Demarchi, Bonnie. In interview with the author. May 7, 2018.
Dreger, Amy, and Aimee Lurie. In interview with the author. July 30, 2018.
Moreau Nicolai, Elizabeth. In phone interview with the author. July 12, 2018.
Trivisonno, Maria. In interview with the author. May 22, 2018.

Websites

China Sprout. Accessed: September 10, 2018. http://www.chinasprout.com.

Connecting for Kids. Accessed: June 29, 2018. https://www.connectingforkids
.org.

Día. Accessed: June 21, 2018. http://dia.ala.org.

Drag Queen Story Hour. Accessed: August 10, 2018. https://www.dragqueensto
ryhour.org.

Jbrary. Accessed: September 10, 2018. https://jbrary.com.

National Council of Teachers of English, National African American Read-In.
Accessed: June 21, 2018. http://www2.ncte.org/get-involved/african-ame
rican-read-in/.

CHAPTER EIGHT

A Parent's Job Is Never Done

When families get to upper elementary and middle school, for the most part, their children are reading fluently on their own. They have found books that they like, and with any luck, they have become library regulars. When this happens, the parents who have been supporting their children start to step back. This is a good thing, but librarians also need to make sure the caregivers realize they still have an important role in the literacy and learning process.

Independent Reader + Parent Reader = Book Conversations

Parents should feel very proud of their kids as they move to fully independent readers. Their kids can read and complete assignments from school without much help from an adult. The role of parents as teacher is not front and center at this point, but parents need not back off completely. There are still ways by which they can continue a reading relationship with their kids.

Reading Together

Continuing to read the same books their kids or teens are reading and having discussions with them about the books opens the lines of communications. Tough and uncomfortable topics can be easier to broach if the conversation stems from a book. Preteens and teens may start putting some distance between themselves and their caregivers, but reading together can help keep the gap from getting too wide.

Listening Together

If the family takes long car trips, listening to audiobooks is another way to keep reading in everyone's life. And now that the kids are a little older, the titles will have more meat to them and will keep everyone entertained. Pausing and discussing what is happening breaks up the hours spent traveling down the road.

Collection Development and Merchandising: Genres

This is a fun age group to work with as librarians and the book suggestions are almost endless. There may still be some talk of reading at a certain level, but it will not be as often. Kids in the upper grades have lots of homework and projects to accomplish during the school year and may be seeking out the library for resources to support their course work. Breaks and summer vacation will likely be the time that they can devote to pleasure reading.

Plan Ahead

Make sure you are paying attention to the school calendars in your area. Noting when the breaks take place can help you decide when to offer programs and to decide what books you add to your displays. Time out of school is very scheduled for today's kids, so making a trip to the library must meet or exceed caregiver expectations. If you are able to do this, it will likely earn you a repeat visit the next time they have time off.

Displays

If you can, stock up on new copies of favorite authors and series before the deluge happens. Make the fresh copies into a display in a prominent location. Surprise and delight families by having what they are looking for in the library. When that is not an option and every Jeff Kinney or Lincoln Pierce book is checked out, have a list of read-a-likes you can recommend.

Readers Advisory

School breaks are also when you will want to have all your favorite new books at the ready to recommend. Free time will mean time to try out new series and authors. Creating a display of titles picked by staff can really help. You can go through your reading history and pull out favorites from the last six months or so to have at the ready. I have used both excel spreadsheets and Goodreads to keep track of what I have read. Find a system that works for you. The longer you work in a library and the more you read, the harder it will be to keep it all straight without something to refer back to.

Reading by the Genres

This is just a small peek at the variety of genres and books that fall into their categories. Start your own list and see how many new genres you can create. Ask your customers and students to help you. These lists will help you make recommendations and can even be shared with voracious readers looking for that next perfect read.

Adventure

Eagar, Lindsay. **Race to the Bottom of the Sea**. Somerville, MA: Candlewick Press, 2017. 423p. $17.99. 9780763679231.
   A pirate and the orphan daughter of marine scientists are thrown together in their search for treasure.
White, Wade Albert. **The Adventurer's Guide to Successful Escapes.** Illustrated by Mariano Epelbaum. New York, NY: Little, Brown and Company, 2016. 374p. (The Adventurer's Guide). $16.99. 9780316305280.
   A true hero's quest with two girls leading the charge and solving the clues along the way.

Fantasy

Chokshi, Roshani. **Aru Shah and the End of Time**. New York, NY: Rick Riordan Presents, 2018. 355p. (A Pandava Novel). $16.99. 9781368012355.
   Indian culture and mythology are explored when Aru Shah accidentally releases a demon from a lamp—a demon who could destroy the world.
Dasgupta, Sayantani. **The Serpent's Secret.** Illustrated by Vivienne To. New York, NY: Scholastic Press, 2018. 338p. (Kiranmala and the Kingdom Beyond). $17.99. 9781338185706.
   Kiran's 12th birthday involves her parents disappearing, two princes who sort of come to her rescue, and an alternate world where there is an evil Serpent King.
Shurtliff, Liesl. **Grump: The (Fairly) True Tale of Snow White and the Seven Dwarves**. New York, NY: Alfred A. Knopf, 2018. 295p. $16.99. 9781524717018.
   Who is the fairest in the land? When Grump finds himself caught between the evil queen and her stepdaughter, he discovers they have two very different definitions for fairest in the land.

Historical

Bradley, Kimberly Brubaker. **The War That Saved My Life**. New York, NY: Dial Books for Young Readers, 2015. 316p. $16.99. 9780803740815.
   The start of World War II offers Ada the chance to escape her cruel mother when she and brother Jamie evacuate to the English countryside.
Bruchac, Joseph. **Two Roads**. New York, NY: Dial Books for Young Readers, 2018. 320p. $16.99. 9780735228863.
   During the Great Depression, Cal and his father are hobos riding the rails. Then suddenly Cal learns he is part Indian, and he is sent to live at an Indian Boarding School.
Curtis, Christopher Paul. **The Watsons Go to Birmingham—1963.** New York, NY: Delacorte Press, 1995. 210p. $16.95. 9780385321754.
   It is the 1960s, the era of Jim Crow laws and the Civil Rights Movement. In the midst of it all, a Michigan family is headed South for a head-on collision with history.
Hiranandani, Veera. **The Night Diary.** New York, NY: Dial Books for Young Readers, 2018. 258p. $16.99. 9780735228511.
   In 1947, Nisha and her family become refugees as they flee Pakistan for a new home.

Magical Realism

Callender, Kheryn. **Hurricane Child.** New York, NY: Scholastic Press, 2018. 214p. $17.99. 9781338129304.
   Caroline lives on the island of St. Thomas, and she has always felt like she has bad luck. Now she is seeing a woman in black and no one else sees her. Could she somehow be related to Caroline's missing mother?
Eagar, Lindsay. **Hour of the Bees.** Somerville, MA: Candlewick Press 2016. 360p. $16.99. 9780763679224.
   A grandfather with dementia tells the most fantastical stories about his wife Carolina, but might there be some truth intertwined with the magic?
Kelly, Erin Entrada. **Hello, Universe.** New York, NY: Greenwillow Books, 2017. 311p. $16.99. 9780062414151.
   Virgil ends up at the bottom of an old well when an encounter with a bully goes wrong. His friends search for him, but it will take more than coincidences to follow the few clues left behind.

Mystery

Frederick, Heather Vogel. **Absolutely Truly.** New York, NY: Simon & Schuster Books for Young Readers, 2014. 355p. (A Pumpkin Falls Mystery). $16.99. 9781442429727.
   Set in a small town in New Hampshire, a group of kids solve cozy mysteries together.

Guterson, Ben. **Winterhouse.** Illustrated by Chloe Bristol. New York, NY: Christy
   Ottaviano Books, 2018. 370p. (Winterhouse). $16.99. 9781250123886.
   An orphan ends up staying at the Winterhouse Hotel one winter and she
   stumbles upon a magical mystery to unravel.

Realistic

Korman, Gordon. **Restart.** New York, NY: Scholastic Press, 2017. 243p. $16.99.
   9781338053777.
   Chase's amnesia means he does not remember his bullying behaviors so
   he has the unique opportunity to start fresh.
Magoon, Kekla. **The Season of Styx Malone.** New York, NY: Wendy Lamb
   Books, 2018. 297p. $16.99. 9781524715953.
   Caleb and Bobby Gene are relatively sheltered brothers who make friends
   with foster kid Styx Malone—the kind of kid who is always having an
   adventure.
Medina, Meg. **Merci Suárez Changes Gears.** Somerville, MA: Candlewick
   Press, 2018. 355p. $16.99. 9780763690496.
   Merci doesn't understand what is happening to her Lolo. He is becoming
   more and more forgetful, and from her Abuela on down to her older
   brother, no one wants to tell her what is really happening.
Tan, Susan. **Future Author Extraordinaire.** Illustrated by Dana Wulfekotte.
   New York, NY: Roaring Brook Press, 2017. 250p. (Cilla Lee-Jenkins).
   $16.99. 9781626725515.
   Chinese American Cilla is about to become a big sister and has decided
   to cement her place in her family by becoming a famous author before
   the baby is born.

Scary Stories

Baptiste, Tracey. **The Jumbies.** Chapel Hill, NC: Algonquin Young Readers,
   2015. 234p. $15.95. 9781616204143.
   A Caribbean fairy tale where a yellow-eyed jumbie comes out of the
   woods looking like a woman and must be dealt with by the story's
   heroine.
Beatty, Robert. **Serafina and the Black Cloak.** New York, NY: Disney Hyperion,
   2015. 293p. (Serafina). $16.99. 9781484709016.
   When children start disappearing from the Biltmore Estate, only Serafina
   knows it is related to the Man in the Black Cloak. A spooky forest is the
   backdrop for this chilling story.

Science Fiction

Brallier, Max. **The Last Kids on Earth.** Illustrated by Douglas Holgate. New York,
   NY: Viking, 2015. 225p. (The Last Kids on Earth). $13.99. 9780670016617.

The apocalypse has arrived, and Jack and his fellow teens are left to defend their turf from the monsters and zombies.

Stead, Rebecca. **When You Reach Me.** New York, NY: Wendy Lamb Books, 2009. 199p. $15.99. 9780385737425.
A friendship falling apart, mysterious notes showing up, and time travel. The trail of breadcrumbs the author leaves will make re-reads all the more fun.

Sports

Khan, Hena. **Power Forward.** Illustrated by Sally Wern Comport. New York, NY: Salaam Reads, 2018. 126p. (Zayd Saleem, Chasing the Dream). $16.99. 9781534411982.
A Pakistani American basketball player works hard to make the top team.

Klages, Ellen. **Out of Left Field.** New York, NY: Viking, 2018. 276p. $16.99. 9780425288597.
Katy wants to play Little League Baseball, but in the 1950s, girls are not allowed to play. Research will help her uncover the history of women playing baseball.

Connecting with Parents

For libraries, keeping a relationship with parents as the kids grow up is important. It keeps parents coming back to the library and asking librarians for book recommendation. From book discussions to book lists to families reading together programs—the library has many ways to reach and support caregivers.

Young at Heart Book Discussion—Cuyahoga County Public Library, Ohio, Strongsville Branch

Your library probably offers book discussions for adult customers. You may even offer book discussions for kids. It is less likely that you host a book discussion for adults where the titles discussed are written for a child or teen audience. However, mashing up adults with youth books is an excellent way to support caregivers and keep them reading with their kids.

Background

The Strongsville Branch of Cuyahoga County Public Library has been offering their Young at Heart book discussion since 2002. It started before the current children's librarian, Timothy Protiva, came to work at the branch, and it continues to be a staple program that the children's department presents. I started attending Young at Heart in 2015, while I was on the Newbery Award Committee. I was a fly on the wall as the adults discussed Newbery eligible books that were selected by the Young at Heart presenters. Once my Newbery reading year was over, I was able to become an active discussion participant and still continue to attend each month.

Planning

Since Young at Heart is a favorite of the staff, they take turns planning and presenting each month. This also helps them balance the other programming planning they have to do. The staff select their own books and they contact the collection development department if additional copies are needed. Along with researching the author and information about the chosen book and creating questions, the discussion leader brings in a treat that is purchased with funds from the Friends of the Library. Sometimes the food relates to the books, sometimes it does not. Protiva even finds that long-time participants will bring in food related to the book on occasion.

Young at Heart is a monthly book discussion that meets on the first Tuesday of the month. The discussion starts at 7:00 P.M. and is scheduled for one hour, but most months, it goes closer to an hour and a half. They meet every month except July and December. This gives the staff a little break, and they find the participants are less likely to be able to make it those two months.

Discussion Participants

Some of the adults attending have been coming since the beginning. Several can figure out how long they have been coming simply by the ages of their children. Being a parent is not required, but many of the attendees are parents and grandparents. Some are teachers or retired teachers. A few are school librarians or retired school librarians. And some are just adults who like to read kid's books. For those with children in their lives, they are looking for books they can share and talk about with them. On average, attendance is between 10 to 15 adults, and most people come on a regular basis.

The diverse backgrounds of the attendees lend itself to lively discussions each month. Just like in any book discussion, there will be strong feelings about a book. Attendees may not like the genre chosen or the style of the author. Frankly, these are some of the best discussions to attend. It is also interesting to see people change their minds about a book based on the evening's discussion.

Selecting Books

The staff at the Strongsville Branch do not shy away from certain types of books or genres. They find that sometimes one fantasy book will work but a different fantasy book will not be liked by attendees. Instead of sticking to specific genres, try these overarching tips for selecting books for discussion with adults.

• Pick books that have good character and plot development.
• Choose titles that lend themselves to discussion in a school setting (Protiva 2018).

Trying at Your Library

You will want to advertise through your typical avenues, but you will also need to use word of mouth. Mention the book discussion to adults who come into the children's room. Post flyers by the adult information desk or by the circulation desk and send an e-mail to teachers to invite them.

As you move forward and start to gel as a group, you can start asking for book suggestions. Adults may suggest titles they think would be good picks. It can also be genres that people would like to read. Giving your book discussion participants some ownership is great, but Protiva also recommends that you look for titles outside the suggestions so you can expand attendees' reading choices a little.

For school librarians, a Young at Heart book discussion could be offered to teachers as a way to introduce new titles from the school library collection. Another possibility would be to partner with your public library. To manage workflow, the school librarian could be worked into the presenter pool at the public library. This would give all librarians in the community the opportunity to connect with parents and teachers.

Great Books for Kids—Cuyahoga County Public Library, Ohio

A personal recommendation from your public or school librarian is the most personal way for families to hear about books. When that is not possible, a good book list can be a substitute and still offer books that will appeal to a wide range of readers. Caregivers can work through a book list and find titles to have their kids try out in the search for their next great read.

Background

The Great Books for Kids gift-giving guide has been a staple at Cuyahoga County Public Library since around 2003, but for almost 40 years, the youth staff have been recommending titles for parents, grandparents, and other caring adults to give to the children in their lives through a book list. The ages included have evolved over time and now include recommendations for kids from birth through 18 years of age.

Age-Level Reading Groups

I have played around with the breakdown of ages and landed on the following in 2018: Ages birth–5 (Early Childhood), Ages 6–9 (Elementary School), Ages 10–13 (Middle School), and Ages 14–18 (High School). Each age group is further subdivided into: Ages birth–2 and Ages 3–5; Ages 6–7 and Ages 8–9; Ages 10–11 and Ages 12–13; and Ages 14–15 and Ages 16–18. This helps make sure that there is a good representation across the whole span of ages in each group. On the final list, each age level has 20 titles on it, 10 from each subgroup, for a total of 80 staff recommendations each year.

Book Criteria

Titles included must be high-quality books that would make good gifts, but holiday books are not included. Other criteria used include:

- Appeal to kids and teens in the specific age group assigned.
- Be age-level appropriate for the assigned group.
- Be from a wide variety of genres and viewpoints.
- Represent the wide range of interests kids and teens have.
- Exemplify the diversity of the 48 communities that Cuyahoga County Public Library serves.
- Consider the appeal to the gift giver, not just the receiver.
- Be published between July and June of the following year.

The choice for publishing year was chosen because the list goes to the marketing department in August so that print pieces and the website can be created. Ending in June means that every book included has been read by participants. When creating a list like this, you should not be recommending titles simply by reviews or past works by an author or illustrator. Your library users deserve lists that you have personally vetted.

Participants

If at all possible, you will want a group of readers to help pick the titles. A variety of voices and opinions helps give breadth and depth to any list created. I lead the group of volunteer library staff for Cuyahoga County, which amounts to 20 to 25 readers each year. Staff do not have to work with youth to participate, but they must love reading books for kids and teens. Reading takes place on non-work time, which is part of the reason participation is voluntary.

Participants are required to make eight suggestions during the reading period for the age group they are assigned to. This usually amounts to roughly one recommendation each month. Attendance at a discussion of all suggested titles takes place before voting for a final list, but the discussion meeting is not mandatory. Sometimes branch duties will trump going to the discussion. All who complete their annotated suggestions on the Goodreads' Great Books page are allowed to vote on the final list.

Timeline

December
Leader sends e-mail asking for staff volunteers.

January through June
Readers make suggestions to the Goodreads' Great Books webpage.

July
Everyone has the month to catch up on reading other readers' suggestions.

August
Participants attend discussion meeting, one for each age group, and vote on their top 15 titles per age subgroup.

August
The final list is created by the leader and sent to the marketing and graphics departments for website creation and promotional pieces.

September
Collection development purchases extra copies of titles on the list so branches can create displays.

November
The Great Books for Kids list goes live.

Trying It at Your Library

Reading, suggesting, and talking about books are all things book lovers enjoy doing. Find your readers and you will be on your way to creating a library-sponsored book list. Cuyahoga County is lucky to have in-house graphic designers, marketers, and web creators who can give a polished finish to our list each year. Your lists do not have to be fancy and can be a printed or electronic list. Just make sure you include your library's name and logo so families know the list is from a trusted source.

Public Library. Participants, in helping create a book list, can come from your own branch or can be pulled from multiple branches if you are a larger system.

School Library. If there are multiple school librarians in your district, you could work together on a list. When that is not an option, you can bring teachers onboard to help read and suggest titles.

Breakfast and Books—Friends School of Baltimore, Maryland

Bringing parents into the school library can be a challenge, but school librarian John Scott has found ways to make parents an integral part of the Friends School of Baltimore, an independent pre-K to 12 school. By offering a program for caregivers and students, he makes the school library a destination place.

Background

Scott already encourages family members to use the school library whether they attend the school or not. This openness invites families to seek out the library for book assistance. Taking it a step further, Breakfast and Books sprung from the desire to have a community-focused program at the school library.

Planning

There is very little planning involved with Breakfast and Books. Scott does not read to the kids, and no book must be read ahead of time by families. Instead, families with kids in pre-K through fifth grade are invited to the school library the last Friday of the month, except November, December, and May, to share books together. The program is a half hour in length and takes place before the start of the school day. It also includes serving a light breakfast.

Food. Breakfast is currently being made by the kindergarten class because they are working on a service project. Scott provides coffee for the caregivers. If you do not have a class willing or able to make the breakfast, you could simply pick up donuts, coffee, and juice. The cost of providing breakfast would be something to discuss with your principal and possibly a parent group to see if they could help support. In a school that serves breakfast to students, you could ask that kids be allowed to bring their breakfast to the school library on these special days to help cut down on costs.

Books. The school librarian then just has to have books for the families to read. Creating displays for families to browse from can be helpful, but it can also be fun for families to browse the stacks too.

Location. Every school library setup is going to be different. If you have comfy seating, great. Tables and chairs can work and so can having families sit on the floor together. If your space is not big enough for the group you draw, expand out into the school hallway so that you do not have to turn anyone away.

Public Libraries

Inviting families into the public library to read together is also a great idea. Plan your program for a Saturday morning with a light breakfast or one evening with pizza. Invite families to select books and then find a cozy place around the library to read together. Work with your Friends of the Library or local restaurants to supply the food.

Why Families Reading Together?

Breakfast and Books has become a "valued tradition at our school" (Scott 2018). If you want your community to be a reading community, this is a great place to start, and you do not need to just focus on the younger kids. Reading-together programs can be done with middle grade, middle school, and high school kids too. Offering programs like this communicates to parents that reading aloud to and with their kids should continue through the school years.

Winter Learning Challenge—San Mateo County Libraries, California

A fun way for parents and kids to connect about books is through a reading program or challenge at the library. Whether it is over summer or winter break, the opportunity to read for fun and make regular visits to the library can engage families with kids of different ages and reading levels all at the same time.

Background

Amy Selmi from San Mateo County Libraries was approached by a parent just before winter break would be starting. The mom wondered what the library offered for this time period away from school. The library currently offered a dynamic Summer Learning Challenge but did not have anything in place for the two- to three-week winter break.

Like any smart librarian, this got Selmi thinking about whether there were others who might like a little extra enrichment during the winter months, not just in the summer. So, in 2010 she decided to give it a try and started a Winter Learning Challenge at the Foster City Library. Five years later, the program expanded to all 12 San Mateo County Libraries locations and the Bookmobile.

Important to the development process was to have a program that would be familiar to families who participate in the summer break program but on a much smaller scale. Summer-reading programs take lots of planning and usually a decent budget to pull off. Most libraries do not have the staffing or the budget to add a second elaborate program to their workload. To make it work, Selmi looked to condense the three-month program into one month and to have prizes, but not on the grander scale of the summer. This ended up being the perfect solution for San Mateo County Libraries and parents. Kids now look forward to the Winter Learning Challenge.

Planning

Having expanded the program to all the branches, Selmi now has a small team of library staff helping to plan each year, including Stephanie Saba, a community program supervisor at San Mateo County Libraries. They work with a hired graphic designer to update the PDF log. A sample log is included in Appendix H. A specific theme is not used. Instead, they use the name Winter Learning Challenge. The focus for families participating is reading and educational activities that promote critical reading and comprehension skills. The team polls branches for how many copies of the children's and teen log they want printed. They also put together orders for flyers and posters to help advertise the challenge.

Promotion and Parent Buy-In

In order to reach families, the library promotes the Winter Learning Challenge through local businesses, including program sponsors, who post flyers at their establishments. A branch newsletter highlights the upcoming program, and social media platforms like Instagram and Facebook are used.

When talking to caregivers about signing up their children, librarians make sure to encourage parents with kids who are too little to read. A listener path is included on the log, but many don't realize they can participate unless the librarian mentions it during storytime. For older kids, the librarians talk to parents about using the log as a way for the child to engage in reading and activities over the break to help prevent any backsliding during those off weeks.

The school districts have been a great partner for the library system. Some districts e-mail caregivers about the program and include a link to the log so families can print it off at home if they choose. The schools also give the library staff the opportunity to come in and talk about the program with the students and teachers directly. If desired, copies of the log are also left with the teachers to be sent home with each student.

The Program

There is a simplicity to the Winter Learning Challenge that makes it easy for other libraries, both large and small, to adapt for their own use. The kids are required to read ten books and do two activities during the challenge period while teens need to read three books and do two activities. What participants read is completely up to them, which is a great way to keep reading fun over the break. The activities are slightly more structured but still leave kids an opportunity to be creative in how they complete them. And, the rating system for both books and activities gives kids an outlet for expressing their opinion.

Prizes

Offering a reward for participating in a reading program has become pretty standard for libraries, but San Mateo County Libraries still found ways to keep the emphasis on reading and learning. Each child who participates receives a book for completing the log, and those who finish also have a chance to win a family season pass to an area museum given out at each of the branches. For the teen participants, the prizes are more tech-friendly, like a portable Bluetooth speaker or a Polaroid One-Step Camera.

Participation

In 2010, 53 participants finished the challenge at the initial branch. In 2014, still at one branch, the number jumped to 405 kindergartens through fifth-grade participants and 72 middle and high schoolers. In 2017, with 12 branches, plus the bookmobile participating, the numbers jumped to 1,500 in the birth through fifth-grade range and 332 sixth through twelfth graders.

Making It Happen

To take on this program at your library, you will need to find money in your current budget or seek out funding from grants or donations. Selmi spent about $500 when she was hosting at her single branch. The Friends of the Library were able to cover those costs. Now that it is systemwide, the library budgets about $14,000 to cover materials, prizes, and promotion.

A staple at public libraries, summer reading programs encourage reading and learning, while kids are on a long break from school. Keeping up reading skills helps prevent kids from losing hard-earned skills, while they are away from school. With supporting student learning on a librarian's mind, it is only natural that libraries would start looking at the winter break as an additional opportunity to promote reading and learning for the fun of it. If you offer a similar program for adult readers like Cuyahoga County Public Library does for their Summer Reading Program, you will truly have the whole family reading.

Building Your Readers Advisory Toolbox

The end of a year is a good time to reflect on what your favorite books were. If you rate your books, it can be fun to go back and see which books received your highest ratings. You will likely find that your opinion of some books changes as you read other books throughout the year. In 2018, my top 10 reads were a mix of ages, formats, and genres.

Mary's Top 10 List 2018

1. Alexander, Kwame. **Rebound.** Illustrated by Dawud Anyabwile. Boston, MA: Houghton Mifflin Harcourt, 2018. 414p. $16.99. 9780544868137.
    Told in verse, Chuck Bell spends his summer living with his grandparents while grieving the death of his father and learning to play basketball. (Novel)

2. Andrews, Troy, and Bill Taylor. **The 5 O'Clock Band.** Illustrated by Bryan Collier. New York, NY: Abrams Books for Young Readers, 2018. unpaged. $17.99. 9781419728365.
    An autobiography of Trombone Shorty's childhood band that highlights the music and food of New Orleans. (Picture Book, Nonfiction)

3. Cline-Ransome, Lesa. **Finding Langston.** New York, NY: Holiday House, 2018. $16.99. 9780823439607.
    Set during the Great Migration, Langston has just moved to Chicago, and while grieving the death of his mother, he discovers the poetry of Langston Hughes at the local library. (Novel)

4. Connor, Leslie. **The Truth as Told by Mason Buttle.** New York, NY: Katherine Tegen Books, 2018. 326p. $16.99. 9780062491435.
    See the world through the eyes of Mason, a boy who takes everything at face value. When his best friend dies and another friend goes missing, Mason has to find a way to communicate what really happened. (Novel)

5. Fan, Terry, and Eric Fan. **Ocean Meets Sky.** New York, NY: Simon & Schuster Books for Young Readers, 2018. unpaged. $17.99. 9781481470377.
   While grieving the death and celebrating the life of his grandfather, a young boy seeks the special place they always talked about visiting. (Picture Book)

6. Older, Daniel José. **Dactyl Hill Squad.** New York, NY: Arthur A. Levine Books, 2018. 256p. (Dactyl Hill Squad). $16.99. 9781338268812.
   The Civil War with dinosaurs! When riots break out related to draft policies, Magdalys Roca and her orphan friends become part of the underground Vigilance Committee and work to takedown the evil Riker. (Novel)

7. Schmidt, Gary D. **So Tall Within: Sojourner Truth's Long Walk Toward Freedom.** Illustrated by Daniel Minter. New York, NY: Roaring Brook Press, 2018. unpaged. $18.99. 9781626728721.
   Striking biography about Isabella, the slave who grew up to be Sojourner Truth. A strong, tall, fighter of freedom for all people. The rectangular inset illustrations harken back to slavery but also have a contemporary edge to them. Haunting is the image of a family tree that shows the silhouettes of slaves among the branches. (Picture Book, Nonfiction)

8. Thomas, Jan. **My Friends Make Me Happy!** New York, NY: Houghton Mifflin Harcourt, 2018. unpaged. (Giggle Gang). $9.99. 9780544966550.
   Sheep's riddle will make beginning readers and adults alike laugh as they learn all the words that begin with the letter *F* that do not make Sheep happy. Can you guess the one word that will? (Beginning Reader)

9. Thummler, Brenna. **Sheets.** St. Louis, MO: The Lion Forge, 2018. 238p. $12.99pa. 9781941302675pa.
   Told in graphic format, a middle schooler is helping run the family's laundromat and it is about to go out of business. Then she meets a ghost who just might be able to help turn things around. (Graphic Novel)

10. Woodson, Jacqueline. **The Day You Begin.** Illustrated by Rafael López. New York, NY: Nancy Paulsen Books, 2018. unpaged. $18.99. 9780399246531.
    Woodson explores how we learn, grow, and become connected to others if we share the things that make us who we are. A book that demonstrates diversity and inclusion through its words and art. (Picture Book)

Create Your Own List

- Identify your top 10 books and share with families.

- What you consider the end of the year depends completely on you. It could be the end of the calendar year in December or in May/June for an end of the school-year list.

References

Interviews

Protiva, Timothy. In e-mail interview with the author. September 8, 2018.
Saba, Stephanie. In interview with the author. February 11, 2018.
Scott, John. In e-mail interview with the author. September 2, 2018.
Selmi, Amy. In e-mail interview with the author. February 5 and March 27, 2018.

Websites

"Great Books." Goodreads. Accessed September 30, 2018. https://www.goodreads
    .com/greatbooks.
"Great Books for Kids." Cuyahoga County Public Library. Accessed September 30,
    2018. www.ccplgreatbooksforkids.org.

Partnering with Parents: Putting It into Action

Now that you have read about all the ways you can support parents, care-givers, and kids, you may be feeling a little overwhelmed. There is a lot involved in working with families from birth up through middle school. During this time, children grow and develop as readers and individuals and so do the books, programs, and services libraries offer. The goal of this book is to inspire you to try something new and perhaps outside of your comfort zone.

Programming with Parents in Mind

You and your individual library will not have the time, resources, or energy to adopt every program that is mentioned in this book. However, if you already have a dynamic storytime lineup, you may want to focus your attention on school age programs and think about ways you can invite care-givers in. The program can be a brand-new addition to your repertoire, or it can be a program that is already liked by kids but that will also now include parents.

The other area I would highly encourage you to turn your attention to is diversity and inclusion. As discussed in Chapter 7, you want to make sure that you are welcoming all the members of your community. A good place to start is to partner with members of the community who speak another language in order to offer an additional storytime program like a Chinese storytime or a bilingual program.

When it comes to programming, it is always good to stretch yourself a little and change things up for both you and your families. It keeps storytime and other programs from getting stale. Pick just one area to concentrate on for the year, or if you are feeling very ambitious, pick one area per quarter. Adding a little here and there keeps things manageable and the process fun rather than stressful.

Readers Advisory for the Librarian

When it comes to readers advisory, you will become more confident and better at it the longer you work in a library. That is, if you make an effort to dive into the collection. Taking the time to read books for all the ages you serve will build up your skill set. Each chapter in *Partnering with Parents* offers you a way to become familiar with books related to that particular stage of a child's reading life.

You can use the Readers Advisory Toolbox from each chapter as your guide to help you increase the number of books you are reading as well as the variety. You can also use the annotated books as your own personal reading list. If either of these options feels like too much to tackle, you can start smaller. Perhaps you simply read more on the subject related to a program you have decided to adopt or you can challenge yourself to download your library's e-book app and read your first e-book.

I have a rule: I only recommend books that I have personally read when I am presenting to other librarians or teachers. That also goes for all the books annotated in this book. When making professional recommendations, I feel it is important to test the books out first. Taking this step allows you to make a well-informed endorsement of a title. However, that is not always practical for in-the-moment readers advisory to kids and parents. In these cases, I rely on my knowledge of an author, reviews that I have read, and the recommendations of my colleagues.

My reading goal changes from year to year, but I usually strive for between 500 and 1,000 books per year. I count everything I read, from board books to adult titles. I also include audiobooks. Keeping track of what I am reading and striving to meet a book goal has proven to be a good source of motivation. Consider setting your own personal goal to achieve. Make it realistic to your own busy life, and do not feel bad if you are reading more picture books than longer fiction. I will let you in on a little secret: that is the case for me every year!

Your Action Plan

It is time to stop reading this book and put your new knowledge into practice. Here's a checklist to help you get started.

• Pick one new program to implement.
• Tweak one current program to incorporate parents.

- Select a way to keep track of the books you read.
- Create a reading challenge to increase the volume of books you read.
- Weed your collection so your shelves are full of books in great condition just waiting for their reader.

Happy Reading!

One final note of encouragement. If your recommendation is hesitant, kids will sense it, and it will be a turn-off. If you did not like a book, you can still suggest it to a reader who you think might like it. If you do, make sure you do not start with "I did not like it but I think you will," as it will stop parents and children in their tracks. Instead, focus on the joy of reading and what you think makes the book a good choice for the reader in front of you. When you are enthusiastic and share that excitement with caregivers and children, it will be contagious.

Baby and Me Plan: Every Child Ready to Read, Part 2

Cuyahoga County Public Library

Title of Book/Song/Rhyme	Comments to Adults Related to the Five Practices and Six Literacy Skills
Introductions	
Song: "Wake Up Toes" from *Morning Magic*	
Rhyme: Two Little Red Birds	Literacy Skill: Vocabulary
	When we say this rhyme, we will repeat it a few times. The first verse will introduce the bird names, and the second and third verses will introduce opposites like high/low and fast/slow. This is a fun way to introduce new vocabulary to your baby.
Rhyme: Open Shut Them	
Song: "Baby Hop" from *Diaper Gym: Fun Activities for Babies on the Move*	

(Continued)

(Continued)

Title of Book/Song/Rhyme	Comments to Adults Related to the Five Practices and Six Literacy Skills
Book: *Bedtime, Ted!* by Sophy Henn	Practice: Talk
	The plot of this board book story will likely follow some of the routines babies experience as you get them ready for bed. When you read stories like this, it is a good opportunity to talk with your children about what they are seeing in the book and how it might be the same as or different from their life.
Rhyme: Twinkle, Twinkle Little Star	
Rhyme: Flying Man	
Board Book Set: *Where Is Baby's Home?* by Karen Katz	
Rhyme: Patty Cake	
Closing: Our Hands Say Goodbye	

References

Books

Henn, Sophy. **Bedtime, Ted!** New York, NY: Abrams Appleseed, 2018. unpaged. $8.95. 9781419727573.

Katz, Karen. **Where Is Baby's Home?** New York, NY: Little Simon, 2017. unpaged. $6.99. 9781534400887.

Music

Bartels, Joanie. **Morning Magic.** New York, NY: BMG Music, 1987. $9.99. 755174695728.

Hegner, Pricilla, and Rose Grasselli. **Diaper Gym: Fun Activities for Babies on the Move.** Long Branch, NJ: Kimbo Educational, 1985. $9.95. 0937124095.

Large Print Order, October 2017
Cuyahoga County Public Library

Avi. **The Player King.** Waterville, ME: Thorndike Press Large Print, 2017. 199p. $19.99. 9781432841904.

Curtis, Christopher Paul. **Bud, Not Buddy.** Waterville, ME: Thorndike Press Large Print, 2017 (1999). 278p. $19.99. 9781432838461.

Curtis, Christopher Paul. **The Watsons Go to Birmingham—1963.** Waterville, ME: Thorndike Press Large Print, 2017 (1995). 260p. $20.00. 9781432838447.

Kinney, Jeff. **Cabin Fever.** Waterville, ME: Thorndike Press Large Print, 2017. 229p. (Diary of a Wimpy Kid). $20.99. 9781410498786.

Kinney, Jeff. **Dog Days.** Waterville, ME: Thorndike Press Large Print, 2017. 229p. (Diary of a Wimpy Kid). $20.99. 9781410498748.

Kinney, Jeff. **Double Down.** Waterville, ME: Thorndike Press Large Print, 2017. 229p. (Diary of a Wimpy Kid). $20.99. 9781410498687.

Kinney, Jeff. **The Getaway.** Waterville, ME: Thorndike Press Large Print, 2017. 229p. (Diary of a Wimpy Kid). $20.99. 9781432843724.

Kinney, Jeff. **Greg Heffley's Journal.** Waterville, ME: Thorndike Press Large Print, 2017. 229p. (Diary of a Wimpy Kid). $20.99. 9781410498779.

Kinney, Jeff. **Hard Luck.** Waterville, ME: Thorndike Press Large Print, 2017. 229p. (Diary of a Wimpy Kid). $20.99. 9781410498717.

Kinney, Jeff. **The Last Straw.** Waterville, ME: Thorndike Press Large Print, 2017. 229p. (Diary of a Wimpy Kid). $20.99. 9781410498755.

Kinney, Jeff. **The Long Haul.** Waterville, ME: Thorndike Press Large Print, 2017. 229p. (Diary of a Wimpy Kid). $20.99. 9781410498700.

Kinney, Jeff. **Old School.** Waterville, ME: Thorndike Press Large Print, 2017. 229p. (Diary of a Wimpy Kid). $20.99. 9781410498694.

Kinney, Jeff. **Rodrick Rules.** Waterville, ME: Thorndike Press Large Print, 2017. 229p. (Diary of a Wimpy Kid). $20.99. 9781410498762.

Kinney, Jeff. **The Third Wheel.** Waterville, ME: Thorndike Press Large Print, 2017. 229p. (Diary of a Wimpy Kid). $20.99. 9781410498724.

Kinney, Jeff. **The Ugly Truth.** Waterville, ME: Thorndike Press Large Print, 2017. 229p. (Diary of a Wimpy Kid). $20.99. 9781410498731.

L'Engle, Madeleine. **A Wrinkle in Time.** Waterville, ME: Thorndike Press Large Print, 2017 (1962). 271p. (Time Quintet). $21.99. 9781410499202.

Lewis, C. S. **The Lion, the Witch, and the Wardrobe.** Waterville, ME: Thorndike Press Large Print, 2017 (1950). 217p. (The Chronicles of Narnia). $20.99. 9781410499257.

Palacio, R. J. **Wonder.** Waterville, ME: Thorndike Press Large Print, 2013. 481p. $19.99. 9781410457417.

Rawls, Wilson. **Where the Red Fern Grows: The Story of Two Dogs and a Boy.** Waterville, ME: Thorndike Press Large Print, 2017 (1961). 376p. $19.99. 9781432838454.

Riordan, Rick. **The Battle of the Labyrinth.** Waterville, ME: Thorndike Press Large Print, 2008. 462p. (Percy Jackson and the Olympians). $20.99. 9781410410184.

Riordan, Rick. **The Blood of Olympus.** Waterville, ME: Thorndike Press Large Print, 2014. 657p. (The Heroes of Olympus). $22.99. 9781410472861.

Riordan, Rick. **The Hammer of Thor.** Waterville, ME: Thorndike Press Large Print, 2016. 639p. (Magnus Chase and the Gods of Asgard). $22.99. 9781410492883.

Riordan, Rick. **The House of Hades.** Waterville, ME: Thorndike Press Large Print, 2013. 701p. (The Heroes of Olympus). $22.99. 9781410462039.

Riordan, Rick. **The Last Olympian.** Waterville, ME: Thorndike Press Large Print, 2009. 485p. (Percy Jackson & The Olympians). $20.99. 9781410416780.

Riordan, Rick. **The Lightning Thief.** Waterville, ME: Thorndike Press Large Print, 2006. 483p. (Percy Jackson and the Olympians). $21.95. 9780786282258.

Riordan, Rick. **The Lost Hero.** Waterville, ME: Thorndike Press Large Print, 2010. 707p. (The Heroes of Olympus). $22.99. 9781410433596.

Riordan, Rick. **The Mark of Athena.** Waterville, ME: Thorndike Press Large Print, 2012. 697p. (The Heroes of Olympus). $22.99. 9781410452054.

Riordan, Rick. **The Red Pyramid.** Waterville, ME: Thorndike Press Large Print, 2010. 671p. $20.99. 9781410425362.

Riordan, Rick. **The Sea of Monsters.** Waterville, ME: Thorndike Press Large Print, 2006. 362p. (Percy Jackson and the Olympians). $20.99. 9781410467744.

Riordan, Rick. **The Serpent's Shadow.** Waterville, ME: Thorndike Press Large Print, 2012. 521p. (The Kane Chronicles). $22.99. 9781410447890.

Riordan, Rick. **The Ship of the Dead.** Waterville, ME: Thorndike Press Large Print, 2017. 575p. (Magnus Chase and the Gods of Asgard). $22.99. 9781432841898.

Riordan, Rick. **The Son of Neptune.** Waterville, ME: Thorndike Press Large Print, 2011. 613p. (The Heroes of Olympus). $22.99. 9781410441225.

Riordan, Rick. **The Sword of Summer.** Waterville, ME: Thorndike Press Large Print, 2015. 697p. (Magnus Chase and the Gods of Asgard). $22.99. 9781410483164.

Riordan, Rick. **The Titan's Curse.** Waterville, ME: Thorndike Press Large Print, 2007. 401p. (Percy Jackson & The Olympians). $22.99. 9780786297016.

Rowling, J. K. **Harry Potter and the Chamber of Secrets.** Illustrated by Mary GrandPré. Waterville, ME: Thorndike Press Large Print, 2003 (1999). 464p. (Harry Potter). $26.99. 9780786222735.

Rowling, J. K. **Harry Potter and the Deathly Hallows.** Illustrated by Mary GrandPré. Waterville, ME: Thorndike Press Large Print, 2007. 969p. (Harry Potter). $34.95. 9780786296651.

Rowling, J. K. **Harry Potter and the Goblet of Fire.** Illustrated by Mary GrandPré. Waterville, ME: Thorndike Press Large Print, 2003 (2000). 936p. (Harry Potter). $29.99. 9780786229277.

Rowling, J. K. **Harry Potter and the Half-Blood Prince.** Illustrated by Mary GrandPré. Waterville, ME: Thorndike Press Large Print, 2005. 831p. (Harry Potter). $29.95. 9780786277452.

Rowling, J. K. **Harry Potter and the Order of the Phoenix.** Illustrated by Mary GrandPré. Waterville, ME: Thorndike Press Large Print, 2003. 1231p. (Harry Potter). $29.95. 9780786257782.

Rowling, J. K. **Harry Potter and the Prisoner of Azkaban.** Illustrated by Mary GrandPré. Waterville, ME: Thorndike Press Large Print, 2003 (1999). 591p. (Harry Potter). $26.99. 9780786222742.

Rowling, J. K. **Harry Potter and the Sorcerer's Stone.** Illustrated by Mary GrandPré. Waterville, ME: Thorndike Press Large Print, 1999. 422p. (Harry Potter). $26.99. 9780786222728.

Sachar, Louis. **Holes.** Waterville, ME: Thorndike Press Large Print, 2017 (1998). 289p. $20.99. 9781432841867.

Book Buddies Sample Plan
Cuyahoga County Public Library

Reading Time	Little buddies practice reading. Have two copies of each book so that both big and little buddies can follow along.
Word Game Book	Librarian reads a book that incorporates word play or puns.
	Wumbers by Amy Krouse Rosenthal, illustrated by Tom Lichtenheld.
Literacy Activity	Locomotion Letters—Make flashcards with a word and image for each letter of the alphabet. Buddy pairs draw a card and act out what is on the card, while the other kids guess the word. Great way to build vocabulary. For example, C is for Clap or W is for Wave.
Read Aloud	Librarian reads a selection from a chapter book.
	Chocolate Touch by Patrick Skene Catling.

References

Books

Catling, Patrick Skene, and Margot Apple. **Chocolate Touch.** New York, NY: HarperTrophy, 1992 (1979). 126p. $6.99pa. 9780688161330pa.

Rosenthal, Amy Krouse. **Wumbers.** Illustrated by Tom Lichtenheld. San Francisco, CA: Chronicle Books, 2012. unpaged. $16.99. 9781452110226.

Family Graphic Novel Book Group, *Little White Duck* 4th–5th Grade Discussion Questions

Multnomah County Library

Reprinted with permission from Natasha Forrester Campbell, Multnomah County Library.

Give the book your secret rating!

Does anyone have a 10-word summary?

Elements for discussion this month:

- *Art technique*: art style—Cartoonish? Realistic? Manga-influenced? Primitive?
- *Literary technique*: Talk about the conflict—what problem or issue needs to be addressed or solved within the plot?

Da Qin = dah tzchooeen (or tzchween)

Xiao Qin = sha-ouh tzchooween (or tzchween)

General questions—pick and choose those most appropriate to the title under discussion:

- How did you read the story? Words then pictures? Pictures then words? All the pictures then all the words? Does it make a difference?

- What connected for you in this book—what things reminded you of your own real life or things you've seen or done?
- This is our first nonfiction book—this is called a memoir. Anyone know what that is?
- It's basically several short stories from the author's childhood—was there one that you especially liked? Any that you didn't like?

    - What was the saddest/funniest/scariest/most exciting part of the story?
    - What would you do if you were in that situation?
    - Rice story—Do you have stories in your family of something that happened to a parent or grandparent and that's why you don't do something or should do something?

- Why do you think the author decided to make this a graphic novel instead of a chapter book?

    - What kinds of things happen in the pictures that don't happen in the text?

        - Look at pages 90–91—talk with your family about what you can tell from the pictures that aren't in the words and vice versa; does that information work together?

    - Were there parts you'd rather have read in a chapter book without the pictures?

- What do you notice about the art style (color, line, style, etc.)?

    - Would you describe the style as cartoonish (exaggerated version of reality)? Realistic? Manga-influenced? Primitive/naive—like a child or someone without any training?
    - How do the panels fit together (overlapping? are there panels?)? Does that tell you anything about the story?
    - What about the color choices? Color palettes can represent a time in history or a memory.
    - Are the *words* themselves or the speech bubbles written or drawn in ways that add to the story? (sound effects, adding emotion, etc.)

- Was there anything in this book that was unfamiliar to you such as a real place you'd never heard of? Did you discuss new vocabulary words with your grown-up or look them up in the dictionary?
- Have you read anything that reminded you of this book?
- Would you recommend this book to your friends?

Chinese New Year 2018—February 16

• Author and illustrator interview: www.slj.com/2012/10/books-media/a-childs-eye-view-of-china-interview/

Did you know you can learn Mandarin through the library's online service, Mango Connect?!?
Chinese pronunciation wiki: https://resources.allsetlearning.com/chinese/pronunciation/Pronunciation_points_by_level
Chinese origami craft:

• Red envelope: www.youtube.com/watch?v=KqUTt-nJzpo

Snacks:

• Popcorn—Da Quin's father sold popcorn when he was in school
• Rice—puffed rice cereal or rice cakes
• Tofu balls
• Kelp—seaweed snacks
• Raspberries—there's a raspberry tree on pages 68–69!
• Chocolate gold coins for the red envelopes

Reference

Book

Liu, Na. **Little White Duck.** Illustrated by Andrés Vera Martínez. Minneapolis, MN: Graphic Universe, 2012. 108p. $9.99pa. 9780761381150pa.

Predicting the 2018 Caldecott Winner

Dayton Metro Library

Reprinted with permission from Melissa Sokol.

After you look through the art of one of the picture books, rate it on a scale of 1–10 for how much you enjoyed the art and jot down any notes or thoughts you had about the artwork.

Things to consider:

- Can the pictures tell a story on their own without the text?
- Is the artwork unique? Something you have never seen before?

1. *Noisy Night* by Mac Barnett, illustrated by Brian Briggs
2. *Grand Canyon* by Jason Chin
3. *Big Cat, Little Cat* by Elisha Cooper
4. *Wolf in the Snow* by Matthew Cordell
5. *Jabari Jumps* by Gaia Cornwall
6. *The Legend of Rock Paper Scissors* by Drew Daywalt, illustrated by Adam Rex
7. *This House, Once* by Deborah Freedman
8. *Lucia the Luchadora* by Cynthia Leonor Garza, illustrated by Alyssa Bermudez
9. *Hello Goodbye Dog* by Maria Gianferrari, illustrated by Patrice Barton
10. *Little Fox in the Forest* by Stephanie Graegin
11. *Egg* by Kevin Henkes
12. *Be Quiet* by Ryan T. Higgins

13. *All Ears, All Eyes* by Richard Jackson, illustrated by Katherine Tillotson

14. *A Greyhound, A Groundhog* by Emily Jenkins, illustrated by Chris Applehans

15. *The Book of Mistakes* by Corinna Luyken

16. *Mama Lion Wins the Race* by Jon J. Muth

17. *Blue Sky White Stars* by Sarvinder Naberhaus, illustrated by Kadir Nelson

18. *The Three Billy Goats Gruff* by Jerry Pinkney

19. *Niko Draws a Feeling* by Bob Raczka, illustrated by Simone Shin

20. *Round* by Joyce Sidman, illustrated by Taeeum Yoo

References

Books

Barnett, Mac. **Noisy Night.** Illustrated by Brian Biggs. New York, NY: Roaring Brook Press, 2017. unpaged. $23.99. 9781596439672.

Chin, Jason. **Grand Canyon.** New York, NY: A Neal Porter Book, 2017. unpaged. $19.99. 9781596439504.

Cooper, Elisha. **Big Cat, Little Cat.** New York, NY: Roaring Brook Press, 2017. unpaged. $16.99. 9781626723719.

Cordell, Matthew. **Wolf in the Snow.** New York, NY: Feiwel and Friends, 2017. unpaged. $17.99. 9781250076366.

Cornwall, Gaia. **Jabari Jumps.** New York, NY: 2017. unpaged. $15.99. 978076 3678388.

Daywalt, Drew. **The Legend of Rock Paper Scissors.** Illustrated by Adam Rex. New York, NY: Balzer + Bray, 2017. unpaged. $17.99. 9780062438898.

Freedman, Deborah. **This House, Once.** New York, NY: Atheneum Books for Young Readers, 2017. unpaged. $17.99. 9781481442848.

Garza, Cynthia Leonor. **Lucía the Luchadora.** Illustrated by Alyssa Bermudez. Brooklyn, NY: Pow!, 2017. unpaged. $16.99. 9781576878279.

Gianferrari, Maria. **Hello Goodbye Dog.** Illustrated by Patrice Barton. New York, NY: Roaring Brook Press, 2017. unpaged. $16.99. 9781626721777.

Graegin, Stephanie. **Little Fox in the Forest.** New York, NY: Schwartz & Wade Books, 2017. unpaged. $17.99. 9780553537895.

Henkes, Kevin. **Egg.** New York, NY: Greenwillow Books, 2017. unpaged. $17.99. 9780062408723.

Higgins, Ryan T. **Be Quiet.** New York, NY: Disney Hyperion, 2017. unpaged. $17.99. 9781484731628.

Jackson, Richard. **All Ears, All Eyes.** Illustrated by Katherine Tillotson. New York, NY: A Caitlyn Dlouhy Books, 2017. unpaged. $17.99. 9781481415712.

Jenkins, Emily. **A Greyhound A Groundhog.** Illustrated by Chris Applehans. New York, NY: Schwartz & Wade Books, 2017. unpaged. $17.99. 9780553498059.

Luyken, Corinna. **The Book of Mistakes.** New York, NY: Dial Books for Young Readers, 2017. unpaged. $18.99. 9780735227927.

Muth, Jon J. **Mama Lion Wins the Race.** New York, NY: Scholastic Press, 2017. unpaged. $17.99. 9780545852821.

Naberhaus, Sarvinder. **Blue Sky White Stars.** Illustrated by Kadir Nelson. New York, NY: Dial Books for Young Readers, 2017. unpaged. $17.99. 9780 803737006.

Pinkney, Jerry. **The Three Billy Goats Gruff.** New York, NY: Little Brown and Company, 2017. unpaged. $17.99. 9780316341578.

Raczka, Bob. **Niko Draws a Feeling.** Illustrated by Simone Shin. Minneapolis, MN: Carolrhoda Books, 2017. unpaged. $17.99. 9781467798433.

Sidman, Joyce. **Round.** Illustrated by Taeeum Yoo. Boston, MA: Houghton Mifflin Harcourt, 2017. unpaged. $17.99. 9780544387614.

50 Book Challenge

Euclid Public Library

Expand your reading with the 50 Book Challenge!

- There is no time limit to complete the challenge, just read and enjoy!

- When you've read a book, visit the Children's Library to answer one question about the book to prove that you read it.

- We'll keep track of your progress for you.

- You'll be rewarded for your reading excitement when you've read 10, 25, 35, and 45 books with a grand prize of a Euclid Public Library t-shirt once you've read 50 books!

- Only books on the list will be considered for the 50 Book Challenge.

- We will add more books to the list as the program grows so stay tuned for new additions.

The 50 Book Challenge is great for readers who want to branch out and read new things as well as to encourage reading in readers who need a little help!

the Kids
Euclid Public Library
Youth Services Department • (216) 261-5300 ext. 450

○ *Stef Soto, Taco Queen* by Jennifer Torres

○ *Stepping on the Cracks* by Mary Downing Hahn

○ *Sugar* by Jewell Parker Rhodes

○ *Terrible Typhoid Mary: A True Story About the Deadliest Cook in America* by Susan Campbell Bartoletti

○ *The Toothpaste Millionaire* by Jean Merrill

○ *Trouble with Cheating* by Blake Hoena

○ *Tuck Everlasting* by Natalie Babbitt

○ *Two Naomis* by Olugbemisola Rhuday-Perkovich

○ *Unbound* by Ann E. Burg

○ *Under Their Skin* by Margaret Peterson Haddix

○ *Vicka For President* by Julie Bowe

○ *The War That Saved My Life* by Kimberly Brubaker Bradley

○ *The Watsons Go to Birmingham – 1963* by Christopher Paul Curtis

○ *The Way to Bea* by Kat Yeh

○ *Whatever After: Sink or Swim* by Sarah Mlynowski

○ *Who Was Babe Ruth?* by Joan Holub

○ *Whoosh! Lonnie Johnson's Super-Soaking Stream of Inventions* by Chris Barton

○ *Wishtree* by Katherine Applegate

○ *Wolf Hollow* by Lauren Wolk

○ *Wonder* by R.J. Palacio

○ *Wonder Woman* (Super Hero High Series) by Lisa Yee

○ *A Wrinkle in Time* by Madeleine L'Engle

○ *A Year Down Yonder* by Richard Peck

- *Ahimsa* by Supriya Kelkar
- *All of the Above* by Shelley Pearsall
- *All Rise for the Honorable Perry T. Cook* by Leslie Connor
- *Amber Brown is Not a Crayon* by Paula Danziger
- *Amina's Voice* by Hena Khan
- *As Brave As You* by Jason Reynolds
- *Bear Rescue, True-Life Stories* by Jess French
- *The Best Christmas Pageant Ever* by Barbara Robinson
- *The Best Man* by Richard Peck
- *Beyond the Bright Sea* by Lauren Wolk
- *Bad Kitty Takes the Test* by Nick Bruel
- *A Boy Called Bat* by Elana K. Arnold
- *Brown Girl Dreaming* by Jacqueline Woodson
- *Circus Mirandus* by Cassie Beasley
- *Clayton Bird Goes Underground* by Rita Williams-Garcia
- *Crenshaw* by Katherine Applegate
- *Crossover* by Kwame Alexander
- *Dark Life* by Kat Falls
- *Dear Mr. Henshaw* by Beverly Cleary
- *Deenie* by Judy Blume
- *Diary of a Wimpy Kid: Double Down* by Jeff Kinney
- *Diary of a Wimpy Kid: The Ugly Truth* by Jeff Kinney
- *Dinosaurs Before Dark* (Magic Tree House #1) by Mary Pope Osborne
- *A Dog Called Homeless* by Sarah Lean

- *Dork Diaries: Tales from a Not-So-Secret Crush Catastrophe* by Rachel Renee Russell
- *The Epic Fail of Arturo Zamora* by Pablo Cartaya
- *The First Rule of Punk* by Celia C. Perez
- *Flat Stanley* by Jeff Brown
- *Funny Girl* edited by Betsy Bird
- *George* by Alex Gino
- *The Girl Who Could Fly* by Victoria Forester
- *The Girl Who Drank the Moon* by Kelly Barnhill
- *The Graveyard Book* by Neil Gaiman
- *Hello, Universe* by Erin Estrada Kelly
- *Hero Two Doors Down* by Sharon Robinson
- *Holes* by Louis Sachar
- *The Hundred Dresses* by Eleanor Estes
- *Hurricane Child* by Kheryn Callender
- *I Am Malala* by Malala Yousafzai
- *I Dissent – Ruth Bader Ginsburg* by Debbie Levy
- *I Survived the Great Chicago Fire* by Lauren Tarshis
- *Ignite Your Spark: Discovering Who You Are from the Inside Out* by Patricia Wooster
- *Inside Out and Back Again* by Tranhha Lai
- *Insignificant Events in the Life of a Cactus* by Dusti Bowling
- *The Invention of Hugo Cabret* by Brian Selznick
- *It's Not The End of The World* by Judy Blume
- *Jaden Toussaint, The Greatest – Episode 1: The Quest for Screen Time* by Marti Dumas
- *Jubilee* by Patricia Reilly Giff
- *Just Dance* by Patricia MacLachlan

- *Just Fly Away* by Andrew McCarthy
- *King of the Bench: No Fear* by Steve Moore
- *The Land of Forgotten Girls* by Erin Entrada Kelly
- *Laura Ingalls is Ruining My Life* by Shelley Tougas
- *Lucky Broken Girl* by Ruth Behar
- *The Marvelwood Magicians* by Diane Zahler
- *Matilda* by Roald Dahl
- *The Misadventures of Max Crumbly: Middle School Mayhem* by Rachel Renee Russell
- *Mockingbird* by Kathryn Erskine
- *Monster* by Walter Dean Myers
- *Mustaches for Maddie* by Chad Morris
- *My Night in the Planetarium* by Innosanto Nagara
- *No Talking* by Andrew Clements
- *One Good Thing About America* by Ruth Freeman
- *The Other Boy* by M.G. Hennessey
- *Outside Shot* by Fred Bowen
- *Pashmina* by Nidhi Chanani
- *Pax* by Sara Pennypacker
- *The Peculiar Incident on Shady Street* by Lindsay Currie
- *Posted* by John David Anderson
- *Race to the Bottom of the Sea*
- *Rain Reign* by Ann M. Martin
- *Rules* by Cynthia Lord
- *Sarah, Plain and Tall* by Patricia MacLachlan
- *Save Me a Seat* by Gita Varadarajan and Sarah Weeks
- *See You in the Cosmos* by Jack Cheng
- *Short* by Holly Goldberg Sloan
- *Some Writer: The Story of E.B. White* by Melissa Sweet

References

Alexander, Kwame. **The Crossover.** Boston, MA: Houghton Mifflin Harcourt, 2014. 237p. $16.99. 9780544107717.

Anderson, John David. **Posted.** New York, NY: Walden Pond Press, 2017. 369p. $16.99. 9780062338204.

Applegate, Katherine. **Crenshaw.** New York, NY: Feiwel and Friends, 2015. 245p. $16.99. 9781250043238.

Applegate, Katherine. **Wishtree.** Illustrated by Charles Santoso. New York, NY: Feiwel and Friends, 2017. 215p. $16.99. 9781250043221.

Arnold, Elana K. **A Boy Called Bat.** Illustrated by Charles Santoso. New York, NY: Walden Pond Press, 2017. 198p. (Bat). $16.99. 9780062445827.

Babbitt, Natalie. **Tuck Everlasting.** New York, NY: Farrar, Straus, Giroux, 1975. 139p. $16.95. 9780374378486.

Barnhill, Kelly. **The Girl Who Drank the Moon.** Chapel Hill, NC: Algonquin Young Readers, 2016. 386p. $16.95. 9781616205676.

Barrtoletti, Susan Campbell. **Terrible Typhoid Mary: A True Story of the Deadliest Cook in America.** Boston, MA: Houghton Mifflin Harcourt, 2015. 229p. $17.99. 9780544313675.

Barton, Chris. **Whoosh!: Lonnie Johnson's Super-Soaking Stream of Inventions.** Illustrated by Don Tate. Watertown, MA: Charlesbridge, 2016. unpaged. $16.95. 9781580892971.

Beasley, Cassie. **Circus Mirandus.** Illustrated by Diana Sudyka. New York, NY: Dial Books for Young Readers, 2015. 292p. $17.99. 9780525428435.

Behar, Ruth. **Lucky Broken Girl.** New York, NY: Nancy Paulsen Books, 2017. 243p. $16.99. 9780399546440.

Bird, Betsy, ed. **Funny Girl: Funniest. Stories. Ever.** New York, NY: Viking, 2017. 205p. $16.99. 9780451477316.

Blume, Judy. **Deenie.** New York, NY: A Richard Jackson Book, 2003 (1973). 156p. $17.99. 9781481414418.

Blume, Judy. **It's Not the End of the World.** New York, NY: A Richard Jackson Book, 2003 (1972). 211p. $17.99. 9781481414357.

Bowe, Julie. **Vicka for President.** North Mankato, MN: Stone Arch Books, 2017. 148p. (Victoria Torres, Unfortunately Average). $5.95pa. 9781496538086pa.

Bowen, Fred. **Outside Shot.** Atlanta, GA: Peachtree, 2017. 133p. (Fred Bowen Sports Story). $6.95pa. 9781561459568pa.

Bowling, Dusti. **Insignificant Events in the Life of a Cactus.** New York, NY: Sterling Children's Books, 2017. 262p. $14.95. 9781454923459.

Bradley, Kimberly Brubaker. **The War That Saved My Life.** New York, NY: Dial Books for Young Readers, 2015. 316p. $16.99. 9780803740815.

Brown, Jeff. **Flat Stanley His Original Adventure!** Illustrated by Macky Pamintuan. New York, NY: Harper, 1992 (1964). 72p. (Flat Stanley). $13.99. 9781442012721.

Bruel, Nick. **Bad Kitty Takes the Test.** New York, NY: A Neal Porter Book, 2017. 144p. (Bad Kitty). $13.99. 9781626725898.

Burg, Ann E. **Unbound: A Novel in Verse.** New York, NY: Scholastic, 2016. 345p. $16.99. 9780545934275.

Callender, Kheryn. **Hurricane Child.** New York, NY: Scholastic Press, 2018. 214p. $17.99. 9781338129304.

Cartaya, Pablo. **The Epic Fail of Arturo Zamora.** New York, NY: Viking, 2017. 236p. $16.99. 9781101997239.

Chanani, Nidhi. **Pashmina.** New York, NY: First Second, 2017. 169p. $16.99pa. 9781626720879pa.

Cheng, Jack. **See You in the Cosmos.** New York, NY: Dial Books for Young Readers, 2017. 314p. $16.99. 9780399186370.

Cleary, Beverly. **Dear Mr. Henshaw.** Illustrated by Paul O. Zelinsky. New York, NY: Morrow Junior Books, 1983. 134p. $16.99. 9780688024055.

Clements, Andrew. **No Talking.** Illustrated by Mark Elliott. New York, NY: Atheneum Books for Young Readers, 2009 (2007). 146p. $5.99pa. 9781416909842pa.

Connor, Leslie. **All Rise for the Honorable Perry T. Cook.** New York, NY: Katherine Tegan Books, 2016. 382p. $16.99. 9780062333469.

Currie, Lindsay. **The Peculiar Incident on Shady Street.** New York, NY: Aladdin, 2017. 295p. $16.99. 9781481477048.

Curtis, Christopher Paul. **The Watsons Go to Birmingham—1963.** New York, NY: Delacorte Press, 1995. 210p. $16.95. 9780385321754.

Dahl, Roald. **Matilda.** Illustrated by Quentin Blake. New York, NY: Viking, 1988. 234p. $16.99. 9780670824397.

Danziger, Paula. **Amber Brown Is Not a Crayon.** Illustrated by Tony Ross. New York, NY: G.P. Putnam's Sons, 1994. 80p. (Amber Brown). $16.99. 9780 399225093.

Dumas, Marti. **The Quest for Screen Time.** Illustrated by Marie Muravski. New Orleans, LA: Plum Street Press, 2015. 48p. (Jaden Toussaint, The Greatest). $5.99pa. 9781943169016pa.

Eagar, Lindsay. **Race to the Bottom of the Sea.** Somerville, MA: Candlewick Press, 2017. 423p. $17.99. 9780763679231.

Erskine, Kathryn. **Mockingbird.** New York, NY: Philomel Books, 2010. 235p. $15.99. 9780399252648.

Estes, Eleanor. **The Hundred Dresses.** Illustrated by Louis Slobodkin. Orlando, FL: Harcourt Inc., 2004 (1972). 80p. $16.99. 9780152051709.

Falls, Kat. **Dark Life.** New York, NY: Scholastic Press, 2010. 297p. $16.99. 9780545178143.

Forester, Victoria. **The Girl Who Could Fly.** New York, NY: Square Fish, 2010 (2008). 329p. $6.99pa. 9780312602383pa.

Freedman, Ruth. **One Good Thing About America.** New York, NY: Holiday House, 2017. 152p. $16.95. 9780823436958.

French, Jess, and Virginia McKenna. **Bear Rescue.** Hauppauge, NY: Barron's Educational Series, Inc., 2017. 89p. (True-Life Stories). $6.99pa. 978143 8010878pa.

Gaiman, Neil. **The Graveyard Book.** Illustrated by Dave McKean. New York, NY: HarperCollins Publishers, 2008. 312p. $17.99. 9780060530921.

Giff, Patricia Reilly. **Jubilee.** New York, NY: Wendy Lamb Books, 2016. 149p. $16.99. 9780385744867.

Gino, Alex. **George.** New York: Scholastic Press, 2015. 195p. $16.99. 978054 5812542.

Haddix, Margaret Peterson. **Under Their Skin.** New York, NY: Simon & Schuster Books for Young Readers, 2016. 311p. $16.99. 9781481417587.

Hahn, Mary Downing. **Stepping on the Cracks.** New York, NY: Clarion Books, 1991. 216p. $16.00. 9780395585078.

Hennessey, M. G. **The Other Boy.** Illustrated by Sfé R. Monster. New York, NY: Harper, 2016. 234p. $16.99. 9780062427663.

Hoena, Blake. **Trouble with Cheating.** Illustrated by Dana Regan. Mankato, MN: The Child's World, 2015. 48p. (Jess & Jaylen). $27.07. 9781631 434426.

Holub, Joan. **Who Was Babe Ruth?** Illustrated by Ten Hammond. New York, NY: Grosset & Dunlap, 2012. 105p. (Who Was). $4.99pa. 97804484 55860pa.

Kelkar, Supriya. **Ahimsa.** New York, NY: Tu Books, 2017. 307p. $18.95. 9781620143568.

Kelly, Erin Entrada. **Hello, Universe.** New York, NY: Greenwillow Books, 2017. 311p. $16.99. 9780062414151.

Kelly, Erin Entrada. **The Land of Forgotten Girls.** New York, NY: Greenwillow Books, 2016. 299p. $16.99. 9780062238641.

Khan, Hena. **Amina's Voice.** New York, NY: Salaam Reads, 2017. 197p. $16.99. 9781481492065.

Kinney, Jeff. **Double Down.** New York, NY: Amulet Books, 2016. (Diary of a Wimpy Kid). 217p. $13.95. 9781419723445.

Kinney, Jeff. **The Ugly Truth.** New York, NY: Amulet Books, 2010. 217p. (Diary of a Wimpy Kid). $13.95. 9780810984912.

Lai, Thanhha. **Inside Out & Back Again.** New York, NY: Harper, 2011. 262p. $15.99. 9780061962783.

Lean, Sarah. **A Dog Called Homeless.** New York, NY: Katherine Tegen Books, 2012. 202p. $16.99. 9780062122209.

L'Engle, Madeleine. **A Wrinkle in Time.** New York, NY: Farrar, Straus and Giroux, 1962. 203p. $17.99. 9780374386139.

Levy, Debbie. **I Dissent: Ruth Bader Ginsburg Makes Her Mark.** Illustrated by Elizabeth Baddeley. New York, NY: Simon & Schuster Books for Young Readers, 2016. unpaged. $17.99. 9781481465595.

Lord, Cynthia. **Rules.** New York, NY: Scholastic Press, 2006. 200p. $15.99. 9780439443821.

MacLachlan, Patricia. **Just Dance.** New York, NY: Margaret K. McElderry Books, 2017. 116p. $15.99. 9781481472524.

MacLachlan, Patricia. **Sarah, Plain and Tall.** New York, NY: A Charlotte Zolotow Book, 1985. 58p. $15.99. 9780060241018.

Martin, Ann M. **Rain Reign.** New York, NY: Feiwell and Friends, 2014. 223p. $16.99. 9780312643003.

McCarthy, Andrew. **Just Fly Away.** Chapel Hill, NC: Algonquin, 2017. 260p. $17.95. 9781616206291.

Merrill, Jean. **The Toothpaste Millionaire.** Boston, MA: Bank Street, 2006. 129p. $16.00. 9780618759248.

Mlynowski, Sarah. **Sink or Swim.** New York, NY: Scholastic Press, 2013. 165p. (Whatever After). $14.99. 9780545415699.

Moore, Steve. **No Fear!** New York, NY: Harper, 2017. 216p. (King of the Bench). $13.99. 9780062203304.

Morris, Chad, and Shelly Brown. **Mustaches for Maddie.** Salt Lake City, UT: Shadow Mountain, 2017. 245p. $16.99. 9781629723303.

Myers, Walter Dean. **Monster.** Illustrated by Christopher Myers. New York, NY: Amistad, 2008 (1999). 281p. $9.99pa. 9780064407311pa.

Nagara, Innosanto. **My Night in the Planetarium.** New York, NY: Seven Stories Press, 2016. unpaged. $17.95. 9781609807009.

Osborne, Mary Pope, and Sal Murdocca. **Dinosaurs Before Dark.** New York, NY: Random House, 2012 (1992). 68p. (Magic Tree House). $4.99pa. 9780679824114pa.

Palacio, R. J. **Wonder.** New York, NY: Alfred A. Knopf, 2012. 315p. $16.99. 9780375869020.

Pearsall, Shelley. **All of the Above: A Novel.** Illustrated by Javaka Steptoe. New York, NY: Little Brown and Company, 2008 (2006). 234p. $8.00pa. 9780316115261pa.

Peck, Richard. **The Best Man.** New York, NY: Dial Books for Young Readers, 2016. 232p. $16.99. 9780803738393.

Peck, Richard. **A Year Down Yonder.** New York, NY: Dial Books for Young Readers, 2000. 130p. $16.99. 9780803725188.

Pennypacker, Sara. **Pax.** Illustrated by Jon Klassen. New York, NY: Balzer + Bray, 2016. 276p. $16.99. 9780062377012.

Pérez, Celia C. **The First Rule of Punk.** New York, NY: Viking, 2017. 310p. $16.99. 9780425290408.

Reynolds, Jason. **As Brave as You.** New York, NY: A Caitlyn Dlouhy Book, 2016. 410p. $16.99. 9781481415903.

Rhodes, Jewell Parker. **Sugar.** New York, NY: Little Brown and Company, 2013. 272p. $7.99pa. 9780316043069pa.

Rhuday-Perkovich, Olugbemisola and Audrey Vernick. **Two Naomis.** New York, NY: Balzer + Bray, 2016. 204p. $16.99. 9780062414250.

Robinson, Barbara. **The Best Christmas Pageant Ever.** Illustrated by Judith Gwyn Brown. New York, NY: HarperCollins Publishers, 1972. 90p. $15.99. 9780060250430.

Robinson, Sharon. **The Hero Two Doors Down: Based on the True Story of Friendship Between a Boy and a Baseball Legend.** New York, NY: Scholastic Press, 2016. 202p. $16.99. 9780545804516.

Russell, Rachel Renée. **Middle School Mayhem.** Illustrated by Nikki Russell. New York, NY: Aladdin, 2017. 228p. (The Misadventures of Max Crumbly). $13.99. 9781481460033.

Russell, Rachel Renée, Nikki Russell, and Erin Russell. **Tales from a Not-so-Secret Crush Catastrophe.** New York, NY: Aladdin, 2017. 256p. (Dork Diaries). $13.99. 9781534405608.

Sachar, Louis. **Holes.** New York, NY: Frances Foster Books, 2008 (1998). 266p. $18.99. 9780374332662.

Selznick, Brian. **The Invention of Hugo Cabret: A Novel in Words and Pictures.** New York, NY: Scholastic Press, 2007. 533p. $24.99. 9780439813785.

Sloan, Holly Goldberg. **Short.** New York, NY: Dial Books for Young Readers, 2017. 296p. $16.99. 9780399186219.

Sweet, Melissa. **Some Writer!: The Story of E.B. White.** Boston, MA: Houghton Mifflin Harcourt, 2016. 161p. $18.99. 9780544319592.

Tarshis, Lauren. **I Survived the Great Chicago Fire, 1871.** Illustrated by Scott Dawson. 96p. (I Survived). $4.99pa. 9780545658461pa.

Torres, Jennifer. **Stef Soto, Taco Queen.** New York, NY: Little Brown and Company, 2017. 166p. $16.99. 9780316306867.

Tougas, Shelley. **Laura Ingalls Is Ruining My Life.** New York, NY: Roaring Brook Press, 2017. 296p. 9781626724181.

Weeks, Sarah. **Save Me a Seat.** Illustrated by Gita Varadarajan. New York, NY: Scholastic Press, 2016. 216p. $16.99. 9780545846608.

Williams-Garcia, Rita, and Frank Morrison. **Clayton Byrd Goes Underground.** New York, NY: Amistad, 2017. 166p. $16.99. 9780062215918.

Wolk, Lauren. **Beyond the Bright Sea.** New York, NY: Dutton Children's Books, 2017. 283p. $16.99. 9781101994856.

Wolk, Lauren. **Wolf Hollow: A Novel.** New York, NY: Dutton Children's Books, 2016. 291p. $16.99. 9781101994825.

Woodson, Jacqueline. **Brown Girl Dreaming.** New York, NY: Nancy Paulsen Books, 2014. 337p. $16.99. 9780399252518.

Wooster, Patricia. **Ignite Your Spark: Discovering Who You Are from the Inside Out.** New York, NY: Simon Pulse, 2017. 215p. $19.99. 9781582705651.

Yee, Lisa. **Wonder Woman at Super Hero High.** New York, NY: Random House, 2016. 237p. (DC Super Hero Girls). $13.99. 9781101940594.

Yeh, Kat. **The Way to Bea.** New York, NY: Little Brown and Company, 2017. 346p. $16.99. 9780316236676.

Yousafzai, Malala, and Patricia McCormick. **I Am Malala: How One Girl Stood Up for Education and Changed the World, Young Readers Edition.** New York, NY: Little Brown and Company 2016 (2014). 240p. $10.99pa. 9780316327916pa.

Zahler, Diane. **The Marvelwood Magicians.** Honesdale, PA: Boyds Mill Press, 2017. 188p. $16.95. 9781629797243.

Adapted Storytime

Cuyahoga County Public Library

North Royalton Branch; In-Branch: May 2018

Theme: Ocean/Sea

Announcements and Schedule

Welcome Song: "New Way to Say Hello" from *Exercise Party: Stretchin' and Jumpin' Songs for Young Children*

Mirror Activity—greet each child and sing a hello song that uses each child's name

Book/Flannel: *Commotion in the Ocean* by Giles Andrae, illustrated by David Wojtowycz (pass out finger puppets)

Song: "Roll with the Waves" from *Rockin' Red* using *scarves* to create movement

Book: *I'm the Biggest Thing in the Ocean* by Kevin Sherry (double visual)

Book: *Breathe* by Scott Magoon (interactive)

Balance Beam Activity with "Balance Beam Song" from *Rocketship Run*

Goodbye Book: *Wave Goodbye* by Rob Reid

Goodbye Song: "Twinkle Twinkle Little Star" from *Catch the Moon* with Gymboree bubbles

Coloring/Play/Social Time—ocean coloring pages and toys from the toy library

---

Reprinted with permission from Angie Bradley, Cuyahoga County Public Library.

References

Books

Andreae, Giles. **Commotion in the Ocean.** Illustrated by David Wojtowyez. Wilton, CT: Tiger Tales, 2001 (1998). unpaged. $14.95. 9781589250000.

Magoon, Scott. **Breathe.** New York: NY: A Paula Wiseman Book, 2014. unpaged. $16.99. 9781442412583.

Reid, Rob. **Wave Goodbye.** Illustrated by Lorraine Williams. New York, NY: Lee & Low Books Inc., 1996. unpaged. $14.95. 9781880000304.

Sherry, Kevin. **I'm the Biggest Thing in the Ocean.** New York, NY: Dial Books for Young Readers, 2007. unpaged. $17.99. 9780803731929.

Music

Laurie Berkner Band, Susie Lampert, and Adam Bernstein. **Rocketship Run.** New York, NY: Two Tomatoes, 2008. $6.99. 695842340621.

Litwin, Eric, and Michael Levine. **Rockin' Red.** United States: The Learning Groove, 2010. $20.98. 884502721089.

Loeb, Lisa, and Elizabeth Mitchell. **Catch the Moon.** Franklin, TN: IndieBlue Music, 2007 (2003). $10.69. 699675199029.

Various Artists. **Exercise Party: Stretchin' and Jumpin' Songs for Young Children.** Toronto, ON: Casablanca Kids, 2007. $8.99. 801464291320.

Winter Reading Challenge

San Mateo County Libraries

Children's Winter Reading Challenge
Reprinted with permission from San Mateo County Libraries.

Read (or listen to) books, comic books, or magazines.
Write down the titles and rate how well you liked them.

Title

1._____ ☆ ☆ ☆ ☆ ☆

2._____ ☆ ☆ ☆ ☆ ☆

3._____ ☆ ☆ ☆ ☆ ☆

4._____ ☆ ☆ ☆ ☆ ☆

5._____ ☆ ☆ ☆ ☆ ☆

6._____ ☆ ☆ ☆ ☆ ☆

7._____ ☆ ☆ ☆ ☆ ☆

8._____ ☆ ☆ ☆ ☆ ☆

9._____ ☆ ☆ ☆ ☆ ☆

10._____ ☆ ☆ ☆ ☆ ☆

Do two new activities and rate how well you enjoyed them.

11._____ ☆ ☆ ☆ ☆ ☆

12._____ ☆ ☆ ☆ ☆ ☆

Turn in your completed log on or before Tuesday, January 16 to get a free
book and enter into a drawing for a museum membership!

Name:_____

School & Grade (if applicable):_____

Phone:_____

San Mateo
County
Libraries

www.smcl.org

Children's Winter Reading Challenge
Reprinted with permission from San Mateo County Libraries.

Teen's Winter Reading Challenge
Reprinted with permission from San Mateo County Libraries.

TEEN WINTER CHALLENGE

Turn in your log on or before January 16, 2018 for a chance to win!

Title

Circle One Emoji

1._____

2._____

3._____

Two new activities

4._____

5._____

Name:_____

Phone number/email:_____

Grade/school:_____

One log per person, suggested for grades 6-12

www.smcl.org

Teen's Winter Reading Challenge
Reprinted with permission from San Mateo County Libraries.

Index

About the Author

Mary Schreiber is the youth collection development specialist at Cuyahoga County Public Library, Parma, Ohio. Prior to that, she was a children's librarian for eight years. She has shared her knowledge about youth services, collection curation, and merchandising at state, national, and international conferences. An active member of the Association for Library Service to Children, she has co-convened the Collection Management Discussion Group and has served on the Theodor Seuss Geisel and John Newbery Medal Award Committees. Her work has appeared in *School Library Journal*, *Children & Libraries*, and the ALSC Blog.